Wonder Anew

A Book of Bible Stories for Adults

Paul J. Gravrock

Fairway Press
Lima, Ohio

WONDER ANEW

FIRST EDITION
Copyright © 2024 by
Paul J. Gravrock

Library of Congress Control Number: 2023922142

ISBN-13: 978-0-7880-4109-9
ISBN-10: 0-7880-4109-6

PRINTED IN USA

To my wife Jean,
without whom this book would not have been completed,
our children and grandchildren would not exist,
and the joy of my life would have been immeasurably diminished.
She is a constant reminder to me that God is truly gracious.

The line drawing on the cover, symbolizing the Triune God, was created by my mother, Lorraine Gravrock, for my ordination on August 30, 1970.

One of the many highlights of this book is clarity! It is one thing to recount an event, it is another thing for the reader to delight in being asked to think when God condemns sin and yet loves the sinner. Gravrock's insightful book is one for teacher, student, and anyone curious about the Bible. His close-to-the bone questions make this book more than just well-worth reading: it's a book for heart, mind, and soul.
Rev. Dr. J.T. Ledbetter, Professor of English, Emeritus
California Lutheran University

Have you ever been invited into a deep conversation? A conversation that caused you to think more deeply about something? This book is such an invitation. It is an invitation – or 80 invitations – into deeper study of some of the most well-known bible stories. The author provides you with the essence of the story, then includes the biblical references so you can explore each one more deeply. Questions at the end of each chapter serve to prompt your inner conversations. If you are curious about the Bible, this book will help you discover its richness.
Rev. Joel S. Wudel, Regional Manager
Mission Investment Fund, ELCA

Wonder Anew *is a faithful retelling of key Bible stories arranged to give the reader a greater sense of the history and interplay of the Christian scriptures. Pastor Gravrock's storytelling can accompany a Bible study, stand on its own as a book study, or serve as a personal devotion guide accessible to clergy and lay people alike. I wish I had this resource for my ministry thirty years ago!*
Rev. Kevin T. Jones, Bishop
Northeastern Iowa Synod, ELCA

In Wonder Anew, *Pastor Paul Gravrock uses scholarship and storytelling to open up well-loved Bible stories for those who might find reading Scripture intimidating or overwhelming. Pastor Gravrock first re-tells the biblical story and then suggests questions for reflection and discussion. I recommend this book for individuals or small group Bible studies who would like to enter the Bible in an accessible and non-threatening way.*
Rev. Shelley Bryan Wee, Bishop
Northwest Washington Synod, ELCA

Paul Gravrock's unique approach to the Biblical narrative offers provocative reflections on eighty Bible stories. He does not retell the stories, but he asks the reader to tackle each one and then think about it—often from an unexpected perspective. At the end of each reflection, he provides a series of questions that lead the reader further into the challenge of connecting the story to one's own life. The result is a book that is part Bible study, part devotional, and part theological reflection. It can be used profitably by an individual, but it would also make a great resource for small groups or Church Council devotions.
Rev. Richard O. Johnson
Editor of *Forum Letter*

When I was a child, I had a favorite set of Bible picture books at my grandmother's house. I remember pulling out these colorful, engaging books and listening to the stories as my grandmother read them to me before I could read them myself. These books gave me a love and awe of God and his word and made me want to know more about him. Wonder Anew *provides a similar feeling. Pastor Paul Gravrock retells the key stories of the Bible in a way that is both engaging and insightful, refreshing understanding and rekindling interest in stories I either haven't read in a while or haven't looked at closely enough. As an addition to regular Bible reading or on its own,* Wonder Anew *provides a beautiful way to see how God is at work in our lives, and understand the whole story of his enduring and faithful love for each of us.*
Dianne Beck,
author of *Sticks and Stones* and *Finding True North*.

Acknowledgements

I do not know of a day in my life in which I did not know the good news of Jesus and the love of God, for from the beginning my parents, Walter and Lorraine, told the Bible's stories to my sisters, Anne and Mary, and to me. As children, we acted out some the stories, and through word and song and works of art we were drawn into the wonder of what God had done from creation to the saving death and resurrection of Jesus. We were taught to shape our lives by these stories and to trust that our lives were part of God's unfolding story.

Jean grew up with the same knowledge and love of Jesus and of the stories of the Bible, so she and I told and retold them to our children, Kari, Sara, and Erik, and then to our grandchildren. Each telling made the stories more precious.

Teachers and professors at every level of my education (public schools in Oxnard and Oakland, California; St. Olaf College in Northfield, Minnesota; Luther Seminary in St. Paul, Minnesota; and San Francisco Theological Seminary in San Anselmo, California) played a vital part in developing in me a love for language, history, truth, imagination, and a deep desire to tell the story of salvation. This was furthered by my seminary internship in an inner-city parish, Grace Lutheran Church in Detroit, Michigan, and by the challenges and joys of my first parish, Grace Lutheran Church in Glendora, California.

I was blessed to serve Good Shepherd Lutheran Church in Novato, California, for thirty-two years, preaching and teaching the story of salvation. During my final three years, I used the adult forum time on Sunday mornings to tell the stories of the people of the Bible. It is thanks to the encouragement of the members of that congregation who heard these stories that they now appear in print.

I am grateful to Jim and Ruth Neumann, dear friends and fellow members of Ascension Lutheran Church in Thousand Oaks, California, for reading the initial draft and for offering insightful and helpful suggestions. Along with Jean, they asked the right questions and offered the right advice to clarify text and intent alike. Their biblical knowledge and grammatical expertise great-ly enhanced the text.

I am also grateful to Dianne Beck, Richard Johnson, Kevin Jones, Jack Ledbetter, Shelley Bryan Wee, and Joel Wudel for reading advance copies of this manuscript and providing feed-back and encouragement.

Thanks are due to David Runk, publisher of CSS Publishing and Fairway Press for his invaluable encouragement and assis-tance in bringing this book to life. Thank you to Becky Allen for editorial expertise, to Publisher's Prepress for formatting, to Ok-erien Emmanuel and Emily Cook for proofreading, and to Olya Vynnychenko for refining the design of the cover.

In it all, thanks be to God for stories worth telling.

Contents

(Stories are told in chronological order.)

Introduction

It is natural to read the Bible with a sense of wonder, but that may mean two quite opposite things.

We may approach the Bible with questions like, "I wonder what all of this means?" or "I wonder how any of this can possibly be true or relate to my life?" or "I wonder if the Bible is worth reading?"

On the other hand, we may come to the Bible with the conviction that what we will find has the power to transform our lives. Such thoughts can fill us with a sense of wonder and of hope.

It is my prayer that this book of Bible Stories For Adults will open your eyes, in the midst of all your wondering, to *see* and to experience true wonder. For the Bible, in all its stories, declares the good news of a God who loves you and who has done everything necessary to restore you to himself.

Bible story books are normally written, it seems, for children. Children are drawn to stories, and stories in turn fuel the imagination of children. The text of a children's Bible story book is augmented with pictures, and young minds are sent spinning into worlds before unimagined.

An adult most often reads books with few if any pictures. The words themselves create the pictures in a mind that has been filled with a lifetime of sights, sounds, and experiences. Yet, too often, all that has been seen, heard, and lived, serves to blunt the imagination and hence the reception of the truth that God intends for us.

One of my seminary professors said that the Bible is often seen as a series of models for morality when, in fact, it is a series of images for identity. In my years of parish ministry, I became convinced that we only understand the wonderful stories of the scriptures when we seek to put ourselves into them, identifying with our forefathers and foremothers in the faith.

When we do this, and when we read the stories honestly, we find that we are challenged and even scandalized by God's word. The stories are not tame and genteel. Some stories, rightly understood, will shock us. But through all of them, we will come to discover the absolute wonder of a God who names, chooses, claims, and loves us.

Hear then the story of the Lord God, the Almighty; and learn that the Bible is true and vital for you as you live your life in this day and in your place.

Textual Notes

Biblical texts quoted, unless otherwise noted, are from the New Revised Standard Version of the Bible (NRSV). A few of the quotes are from the Revised Standard Version of the Bible (RSV), and they are so indicated. These are instances where I prefer the RSV wording to that which is in the NRSV.

Throughout the Old Testament stories (1-37), in line with the NRSV, I have written LORD with all capital letters to indicate that this is God's self-identification to Moses as Yahweh — "I am who I am." (See note below and story number 15.)

Throughout the New Testament stories (40-80), even though it is the same God in both testaments, the designation Lord generally refers to Jesus and is written without using all capital letters. This too follows the practice in the NRSV.

When Bible verses are quoted, the source is indicated as follows: The number following the quote indicates both chapter and verse (even if the particular story is in a single chapter of the Bible). For example, chapter 1 verse 12 is written (1:12) or chapter 39 verses 17-19 is written (39:17-19).

Some of the stories about Jesus are found in more than one of the four gospels (Matthew, Mark, Luke and John). When one account is the focus for the story as told here, that gospel is listed below the title and subtitle, and the citations are understood to refer to that gospel, unless otherwise noted. Below the indicated gospel and in parentheses are the references for the same or similar story in one or more of the other gospels.

Note: The name by which God identified himself to Moses was four Hebrew letters (no vowels) which in English are YHWH (Yahweh). These four letters are called the *Tetragrammaton*. The name was considered to be so holy that it was not spoken except by adding vowels from "Adonai," another name meaning Lord. The resulting name is Jehovah.

1. And God Said...

The Creation, Part 1
Genesis 1

Before there was anything else, there was God. Then God spoke into existence all that is.

On the first day, God said, "Let there be light" (1:3). And it was so. On the second day, God divided the waters and made the sky. On day three, the earth and all vegetation came into being. On day four, the sun, moon, and stars were spoken into being. On day five, the sky was filled with birds and the waters were filled with all swimming creatures. Finally, on day six, the animals were created and people were formed. Six days of creation were followed by a day of rest.

Six days of creation. What are we to make of this? Does this put the Bible in immediate conflict with science? Or is there more here than meets the eye?

The God of all creation is also the Creator of the human mind, and while God urges people to discover all that they can learn, God also remains beyond all that can be known or understood. The job of the scientist is to seek for proof and truth. The person of faith trusts God, both in and beyond that which can be proven.

What about the six days? To believe that God could not have created everything in six literal days (or in a single instant) is to minimize God's power. To believe that what is described could not refer to six eons of time, but must be literally six twenty-four-hour days, is also to minimize God's power. In either case, we are guilty of making God too small.

The first chapter of the Bible is a profound description of three great truths. The first is that God created all that exists in an orderly fashion. The second truth is that God created all things good. The third is that humanity is the crown of God's creation.

The Bible begins with the declaration that God created all that exists. There are no preparatory arguments to prove the existence of God; the creation itself testifies to God's glorious reality. Clearly there is amazing design to the created order. There is diversity almost beyond description, and yet all things work together. This does not speak of happenstance but of glorious design. The conviction of this opening chapter of the Bible is that the designer is none other than God, and the question this raises is humanity's relationship to the designer.

Six times in this opening chapter, God declares that what has been created is good, and the chapter ends with these words, "God saw everything that he had made, and indeed, it was very good" (1:31). Coming forth from the mind and heart of God, the creation was marvelous to behold, and there was perfect harmony. (This is just the beginning of the story, but the conviction is that in the beginning all things were created good.)

Humans, both male and female, are created "in the image of God," (1:27) to be in a special relationship with the Creator. Humans are given the unique ability to respond to God with loving obedience. They are called to "be fruitful and multiply" (1:28). They are given dominion over the creation. Dominion, rightly understood, does not mean domination but rather stewardship. The whole creation, including the people, belongs to God. People are given the authority to act as God's stewards. They are to tend God's creation so that it passes from one generation to another in as good shape as it was received. Care for the environment is as old as the first chapter of the Bible, for so God has spoken.

For thought or discussion:

- God has created the universe with loving care and with a plan for all things. Which aspects of creation cause you to marvel?
- How do your actions give thanks to God for life and for all that exists?
- How do you live out your assignment to be a steward of God's creation?

2. Dearly Beloved

The Creation, Part 2
Genesis 2

This second account of creation focuses on Adam and Eve, the ones to whom God gave stewardship of all the earth.

God intends people to be in a loving relationship with God, with others, and with the created order. "It is not good that the man should be alone," (2:18) God said. God created people for relationship in which they would lovingly reflect God's love. People are not created for isolation but for community. Each person is a wondrous creation of God and is of infinite value. What is true for the one is true for the other, for all are God's dearly beloved.

People are to have a caring relationship with the world and to do all that they can to protect and to enhance it. They are to have a respectful relationship with all living creatures and to cherish the interdependence of all life forms, for truly each needs the other in proper balance for the world to thrive. They are to nourish the life of animals, birds, and those that live in the waters. They are to rejoice in the amazing variety of the created order from the smallest living thing to the vastness of the universe.

Yet it is with humans that there is rightly a special bond, for it is in relationship with other people, in all their diversity, that humans were created to experience and to mirror God's love.

The most unique of all such relationships is to be found in marriage, where a man and a woman come to realize that, by the grace of God, each completes the other. This was God's good and perfect plan. Two people, both in the image of God, were to discover in each other the loving relationship that comes in complete openness and trust. This relationship between husband and wife was to increase the love of each for God and for all that God created. In their partnership, the man and the woman were to mutually tend all of God's perfect creation and to take their place in the chain of the generations, passing on to future generations the knowledge of the God who created them.

In order that life might be rich and full, God placed the people in a setting, the Garden of Eden, that was literally paradise.

In the middle of this garden were the tree of life and the tree of the knowledge of good and evil. Everything was provided and nothing was lacking. There was only peace: with self, with each other, and with the whole creation. All of this was the result of the perfect peace Adam and Eve knew with God.

For thought or discussion:

- How are you living in relationship with all aspects of God's creation?
- What aspects of God's intended harmony do you find most challenging?
- If you are married, do you see God in your spouse?

3. So This Is Perfection?

The Fall / Adam and Eve
Genesis 3

In the first chapter, we learned that God made all things good; yet clearly our experience is that not everything is good. What went wrong?

Adam and Eve lacked nothing, and they experienced only goodness. There was only one prohibition for them: God said, "You may freely eat of every tree of the garden; but of the tree of the knowledge of good and evil you shall not eat, for in the day that you eat of it you shall die" (2:16-17).

Why would there be any restrictions in a perfect setting? Isn't it, in fact, important to know the difference between good and evil? So why would God forbid eating of a tree that promises such knowledge? This is the temptation the serpent placed before the woman. "You will not die;" it said, "for God knows that when you eat of it your eyes will be opened, and you will be like God, knowing good and evil" (3:4-5). The serpent suggested that to have such knowledge was to be God's equal, sharing God's power and being self-sufficient.

Adam and Eve already knew what was good and evil. Everything was good except to disobey God. The temptation was to be the masters of their own lives rather than needing to trust and obey God. Is not this the ultimate temptation people face day after day, wanting to be in charge, not trusting God to be good toward them, and not wanting God to tell them what to do? This rebellion against God is the basis of all sin and brokenness. We call this the fall.

When God spoke to Adam after the fall and asked him, "Where are you?" (3:9), God was not asking about physical location but about the state of Adam's being. Adam's excuse for eating of the fruit of the tree was, "The woman whom you gave to be with me, she gave me fruit from the tree, and I ate" (3:12). Was the relationship between Adam and Eve ever the same after he put the blame on her? And Eve, for her part, tried to pin the blame on the serpent. How "human" it is to think that our improper actions or responses are someone else's fault.

What was the result of Adam and Eve's desire to be in charge? What had been perfect was now distorted. When Adam and Eve rebelled against God's authority, relationship was broken; innocence and holiness were lost. The broken relationship with God caused a fracture of all other relationships: people with creation, person with person, and person with self. The account speaks of the ground being cursed, of life being marked by toil, of pain in childbirth, and of death.

But isn't it all God's fault? If God had not put that tree in the garden and warned against eating its fruit, everything would have been fine. Such thinking causes us to miss this wonderful truth: God did not create humans to be puppets and to love God because they had no option. People could only respond to God in real love if it were possible for them not to do so. In love, God gave people the freedom to choose.

For thought or discussion:

- How do you use your God-given freedom as you make your decisions day by day?
- Where are you experiencing brokenness in the world and in your own life?
- What responsibilities go with having freedom of will?

4. Whatever Happened to Brotherly Love?

Cain and Abel
Genesis 4

Family is intended to be a wonderful thing as each member loves and cares for the other. Alas, it is not always the case. Consider the account of Cain and Abel, the sons of Adam and Eve.

There is no indication that one son was more loved by their parents than the other. There is every reason to believe that both brothers were raised with equal love and kindness.

Cain and Abel had different interests. This is perfectly normal for siblings, and it is a healthy thing that each recognizes his or her own gifts. Cain was a farmer or a gardener, and Abel was a shepherd.

Each brother, in time, chose to bring an offering to the LORD God to give thanks for the success each had experienced. Cain brought an offering of what he had grown. Abel brought an offering from his flock.

God was pleased with Abel's offering but not with Cain's. Is this because God likes sheep more than grain or animals more than plants? Is this some sort of arbitrariness on God's part?

The answer is in the attitudes of the brothers. Abel, it says, "brought of the firstlings of his flock, their fat portions" (4:4). He brought the very best he had to bring. Cain, on the other hand, brought *some* of the fruit of the ground, less than the best he had. God is concerned with the nature of response, for how people act demonstrates the value they place on God.

Cain was angry with Abel for receiving a more positive response from God. Instead of examining his own attitudes, he succumbed to the green-eyed monster of jealousy, and sought to eliminate the one whom he thought made him look bad. He killed his brother, and the brokenness that began with the Fall, poisoned a new generation.

When God asked Cain about Abel, Cain replied with the question, "Am I my brother's keeper?" (4:9). This question rolls through all time as generation after generation comes to grips with the tendency toward hatred. In God's eyes, we are our brothers' and our sisters' keepers.

For thought or discussion:

- How do you deal with conflicts and disagreements that arise in your family or with your friends?
- Has the green-eyed monster ever caused trouble for you?
- How can you be a more caring keeper for those around you?

5. Flood Insurance – Costly but Worth the Price

Noah and the Ark
Genesis 6-9

With the perfection of Eden but a memory, the disobedience of Adam and Eve led to toil, pain, brokenness, jealousy, murder, vengeance, violence, and rampant wickedness. Generation after generation was infected by the sin of rebellion against God. Sin was not merely learned by one generation from the previous one. Sinfulness was now the very mark of humanity, the human condition.

God decided to hit the reset button.

There was one man who, with his family, would become the ongoing source of humanity. His name was Noah. "A righteous man, blameless in his generation; Noah walked with God" (6:9). With his wife and his three sons (Shem, Ham, and Japheth) and their wives, God determined to begin again.

God commanded Noah and his sons to build an ark, a very large boat, and to gather two of each of the animals and birds, male and female, into the ark. Of the animals that would be used for sacrifice to God, there were to be seven pairs, male and female.

Imagine being Noah and receiving such instructions from God. And imagine how it must have looked to Noah's neighbors as he built this huge boat. What ridicule he must have endured. He must have seemed to be a singular fool. No one else wanted to follow his example, and none heeded any warnings he may have sounded.

Two by two, the birds, animals, and creeping things, wild and domestic, entered the ark. They were followed by Noah and his wife, their sons and their wives, a total of eight people. "On that day all the fountains of the great deep burst forth, and the windows of the heavens were opened" (7:11). For forty days and forty nights the rain fell.

All living things on the earth, in whose nostrils was the breath of life, perished in the flood. Only those in the ark remained alive. Here was a floating paradise in which all who remained lived in harmony.

At the end of a year, the ground was again dry and the inhabitants of the ark returned to roam the earth. At God's command, they were once again to be fruitful and multiply.

The first thing that Noah and his family did was to build an altar to the LORD God and to offer pleasing sacrifices to God. Thanksgiving and gratitude were foremost in Noah's mind. And God, in turn, made a covenant that never again would all flesh be destroyed by flood. The sign of this covenant was the rainbow. God made this covenant in spite of knowing that "the inclination of the human heart is evil from youth" (8:21).

It was a new beginning. Yet this new day did not erase the memories of the past or wash away the stain of original sin. The eight people were yet marked by the fall. Therefore, the future they would enjoy would be shaped by their obedience or disobedience to God.

What was true for those eight people who came out of the ark is equally true for us today. Once sin is learned, it passes easily from generation to generation. Faithfulness to God is difficult to live out and to teach, but doing so is the path to a blessed future.

For thought or discussion:

- What do you think about when you see a rainbow?
- How are you a part of God's promise of blessing?
- Why would sin still exist after the "reset" of the flood?
- In the account of the flood, the drying of the land was shown by a dove bearing in its beak a freshly plucked olive leaf. Why has this become a symbol for peace?

6. I Don't Speak Your Language

The Tower of Babel
Genesis 11

Pieter Bruegel the Elder's painting of the Tower of Babel, based on the first nine verses of this chapter, is well known. It portrays people hard at work to build a massive tower reaching into the clouds.

The purpose behind the construction of this tower is described in the words of the planners: "Come, let us build ourselves a city, and a tower with its top in the heavens, and let us make a name for ourselves" (11:4). Here is an echo of the rebellion in Eden. Let us glorify ourselves. Let us make clear to others our own importance. The focus is on self (or one's own community) rather than on God.

To keep the people from getting carried away with their own importance, God confused their language so that they could not easily communicate and carry out their self-aggrandizing project. Then, speaking different languages, the people were scattered over the face of all the earth.

Two things have remained true since that time. The first is the ongoing desire of people to build monuments to call attention to their own importance. Whether it is having the finest house in the community or the fanciest car to drive, the message is the same. Belonging to the right club or having the latest technological device can serve to impress others. A diploma from an elite university, a string of letters or titles before or after one's name, or a wall full of citations will often do the trick. The list goes on and on.

Notice too that there was a time when the tallest structures in towns or cities were the towers or steeples of the churches or cathedrals. While these may well have been built partly to glorify the builders or architects, they nevertheless pointed toward God. Today the tallest and most impressive buildings in most cities are the bank, insurance, or corporation buildings. While there is nothing inherently wrong with banking, insurance, or corporate business, it is arguably true that these buildings point to human accomplishments and power rather than to the glory of God.

The second thing that is true since the days of the Tower of Babel is that language is a barrier that must be overcome if communication is to take place. When we cannot understand the words of another person, we sometimes tend to regard that person with either suspicion or fear. Even when we speak the same language as another person, we can easily misunderstand either the words that are used or the tone of the voice.

Communication is an ongoing challenge. Without clear understanding, community fractures; and fear or hatred divide the human family in the most disastrous of ways.

For thought or discussion:

- What do you consider to be the foremost measure of your worth or importance?
- How have you experienced difficulties caused by language barriers?
- Which are the most impressive buildings in your community?
- Is there a building or structure that especially thrills or inspires you?

7. We're Moving, Dear

Abraham and Sarah
Genesis 12

"Go from your country and your kindred and your father's house to the land the I will show you. I will make of you a great nation, and I will bless you, and make your name great, so that you will be a blessing. I will bless those who bless you, and the one who curses you I will curse; and in you all the families of the earth shall be blessed" (12:1-3). So spoke God to Abraham.

The land in which Abraham (initially Abram) and his wife, Sarah (initially Sarai), lived was polytheistic. This means that the people worshiped a variety of gods. This was quite normal and this is what makes this account so amazing.

Out of the blue, with no apparent introduction, the Lord God spoke to Abraham and gave him an assignment and a promise. Leave your home and family and all that is familiar, then go where I direct you to go. You will be great and blessed and you will become a blessing to the world. Simple enough? Risky? A sure and certain outcome?

What do you think Abraham thought? Should he write this off as a hallucination? Was it something he ate or drank that didn't agree with him?

Whatever Abraham's initial reaction, he did what he was told to do.

First, of course, he had to announce this to Sarah. This may or may not have been good news to her. She may have just finished decorating her home so that it was exactly the way she wanted it to be. She may have had a wonderful circle of friends, and she may well have been very connected in her community. The fact that Abraham was convinced that God had spoken to him could have been dismissed by Sarah as nothing but his imagination.

Whatever Sarah's initial reaction, she did what she was asked to do.

Taking their nephew Lot, their possessions, and their entourage, they left Haran and traveled to the land of Canaan, the land which God showed to them.

Why did God interfere in the settled lives of Abraham and Sarah this way? The answer takes us back to what was said earlier about the land where they had been living. Many different gods were worshiped in Haran and in Canaan, but while the former was familiar territory, the latter was not. God wanted Abraham's undivided attention, and God wanted Abraham and his family to worship only the LORD God. In Haran there would have been too many familiar things calling them back to their old ways. In Canaan, only God was familiar to Abraham and Sarah.

All of this was God's eternal plan to bless and redeem the world. To accomplish this, God chose Abraham and his descendants. Why Abraham? Why ultimately the Jewish people? Perhaps the greater question is, why not? It is what God did, and we will see as the story unfolds that it was, wonder of wonders, the perfect choice.

For thought or discussion:

- What would you think if God spoke to you as God spoke to Abraham?
- Has God ever spoken to you, and if so, how?
- Have you ever been called to take a risk that required you to put your trust in a spoken promise?
- How do our individual actions and decisions impact those who share life with us?

8. Helping God Along

Sarah and Hagar
Genesis 16 and 21

God promised Abraham that he and Sarah would have descendants as numerous as the stars in the heavens or the sand of the seashore. Years passed, and still there were no children for the two of them. What was to be done? Surely God needed help to fulfill the promise.

Sarah had an Egyptian slave-girl named Hagar. Sarah reasoned that, if she herself could not conceive, Hagar could be a surrogate and produce a child to Sarah's credit.

The first part of the plan worked perfectly. Hagar became pregnant. But then Hagar, seeing that she had accomplished what Sarah could not, looked on Sarah with contempt. So much for crediting a child to Sarah. In her anger, disappointment, and jealousy, Sarah treated Hagar harshly, and Hagar ran away.

An angel of the LORD found Hagar in the wilderness and told her to return and submit to her mistress. The angel also told her that she would bear a son whom she was to name Ishmael and promised that she herself would have descendants beyond number.

It came to pass that Hagar bore a son and named him Ishmael. His father, Abraham, was eighty-six-years-old when his son was born.

But there is more to this story.

When Abraham was one hundred years-old and Sarah was ninety, God announced that the two of them would finally have a son of their own. Sarah laughed at the very thought of such nonsense, but it came to pass, and the child born to them was named Isaac (which means one who laughs).

When Isaac was weaned, Sarah saw Ishmael playing with him, and again her jealousy rose to the surface. She demanded of Abraham that Hagar and Ishmael be sent away. As sorely as it grieved Abraham to do this, he obeyed. The pain of this departure was somewhat lessened by the word that God gave to Abraham, "It is through Isaac that offspring shall be named for you. As for the son of the slave woman, I will make a nation of him also, because he is your offspring" (21:12-13).

Isaac was the beginning of the fulfillment of God's promise to make of Abraham and Sarah a great nation. Their attempt to help God led to unnecessary strife and jealousy. It often happens when people think that they are wiser or more clever than God.

For thought or discussion:

- Have you ever become impatient waiting for a promise to be fulfilled?
- Has there been a time when jealousy caused you to act harshly toward someone else?
- How would you have felt if you were Hagar or Ishmael?

9. Sacrifice My Beloved Son?

Abraham and Isaac
Genesis 22

What amazing joy a child can bring to a couple. The birth of a child causes the parents to imagine what future blessings will come to and through that child. Surely Abraham and Sarah had such delight in Isaac, and certainly they had high hopes for their son.

Then, the same God who directed Abraham and Sarah to leave Haran and begin life anew in Canaan, spoke again to Abraham. This time, to test Abraham, God told him to take Isaac to a distant mountain and to offer him to God as a sacrifice.

What sense did this make? What do you suppose Abraham thought of this directive? Did he dare to mention this to Sarah?

Many of the religions of the region practiced child sacrifice. The idea was that if a couple sacrificed their firstborn to their god, that *god* would grant many more children to the couple. Given that idea, it is possible that Abraham's neighbors may have been wondering why he and Sarah had not already done their duty to their God.

It was a three-day journey for Abraham, Isaac, and two servants to go from Beersheba to Mount Moriah. They had the wood for the burnt offering, but they took no lamb. Each day must have been a major test for Abraham as he walked along with his beloved son. No matter how solidly he believed God's promise that through Isaac he would become the father of many nations, Abraham must have wondered how this all fit into God's plan.

When they came to the place to which God had directed them, Abraham and Isaac went up the mountain, Isaac bearing the wood for the sacrifice and Abraham carrying the fire and the knife. Understandably Isaac wondered, "Where is the lamb for a burnt offering?" (22:7). Abraham answered, "God himself will provide the lamb for a burnt offering, my son" (22:8).

Abraham built an altar, placed the wood on it, and then bound Isaac and laid him on top of the wood. What was going through Abraham's mind? What fear must have seized Isaac?

God, knowing that Abraham trusted him completely, stayed Abraham's hand. Instead of Isaac, a ram caught in a thicket became the subject of sacrifice. God had indeed provided. God also reiterated his promise to Abraham that through Isaac, the promised blessing of the world would continue. How joyful the two of them must have been as they descended the mountain. How light their steps must have been as they journeyed home. How delighted Sarah must have been to receive them again.

This account is a foreshadowing of the climactic event that would occur in the fullness of time.

For thought or discussion:

- What is the greatest test you have ever faced?
- Which tests in your life have come from God and which have been of your own making?
- Have you ever been saved from what seemed to be a dire circumstance?

10. *Carpe Diem* (Seize the Day)

Esau and Jacob
Genesis 25 and 27

In due course, Isaac married Rebekah, a kinswoman from the land of Haran. After years of waiting, they had two sons, twins. Esau was born first, and Jacob come right after him, holding onto his brother's heel.

By the law or custom of primogeniture, the firstborn child would receive the lion's share of any inheritance and would receive a special blessing. Other children would share the remainder of the estate and receive minor blessings. Though Esau and Jacob were twins, Esau was the firstborn. And yet, late in Rebekah's pregnancy, God revealed to her that "Two nations are in your womb, and two peoples born of you shall be divided; the one shall be stronger than the other, the elder shall serve the younger" (25:23).

Esau became a skillful hunter and was an outdoorsman. He was his father's favorite, for Isaac was fond of game. Jacob, on the other hand, was more quiet and thoughtful. He was his mother's favorite. Esau was one who lived for the moment. Jacob was more focused on what the future might hold.

It happened that one day when Jacob was cooking stew, Esau came in from the field and was famished. In response to Esau's request for food, Jacob, seizing the moment, said that the price of the stew would be Esau's birthright. Esau's overly dramatic response was "I am about to die; of what use is a birthright to me?" (25:32). Food, for the moment was more important to him than any future inheritance.

That still left the matter of the blessing Esau was to receive from his father. When Isaac was old and nearly blind, he asked Esau to hunt game and prepare a savory dish which Isaac liked. Then Isaac would bless Esau.

Rebekah overheard this conversation, and she seized this moment. She directed Jacob to get two choice kids from the flock so that she could prepare the dish that Isaac liked and have Jacob take it to his father and gain the blessing. Jacob protested that Isaac would know that Jacob was tricking him and would place a curse rather than a blessing on him. Rebekah, however, was not to be dissuaded. She dressed Jacob in Esau's clothing and covered his smooth hands and neck with skin from the kids so that he would feel like his hairy brother.

Jacob flat out lied to his father. Isaac asked him if he was Esau, and twice he said that he was. Though the voice seemed to be Jacob's, the smell of the garments and the hair on the hands were enough to convince Isaac. He ate the savory dish, and then he blessed his son. The fact that Isaac thought he was blessing Esau did not negate the blessing that was spoken to Jacob. A blessing placed on a person could not be revoked.

No sooner had this deception run its course than Esau returned. He prepared a meal for his father and brought it to him. Isaac, in his blind confusion, asked, "'Who are you?' He answered, 'I am your firstborn son, Esau'" (27:32). Then it became clear that Jacob (whose name means he supplants) had deceitfully stolen Esau's blessing. All that was left for Esau was a minor blessing which included the word that "you shall serve your brother" (27:40). Esau hated Jacob.

Perhaps the birthright was fairly purchased, taking advantage of Esau's impetuous nature, but the blessing was outright stolen. Nevertheless, both now belonged to the younger brother. Was Rebekah motivated by the word she remembered from the time of her pregnancy? She certainly orchestrated the deception, but Jacob had to agree and to do it. Once again, the brokenness of relationships is revealed. But also revealed is the importance of living into the promised future rather than merely living for the moment.

For thought and discussion:

- Have you experienced a time when you were treated unfairly?
- How do you balance the importance of living fully each day with the need to plan for the future?
- Have you received a blessing that altered your life or shaped your future?

11. The Trickster Gets Tricked

Jacob, Laban, Leah, and Rachel
Genesis 29-33

In his anger, Esau planned to kill Jacob. Rebekah learned of this, and so with Isaac's blessing, she sent Jacob to Paddan-aram (now southern Turkey) to her brother Laban's home. There he would be safe, and there he would find a wife.

So it was. Jacob fell madly in love with Rachel, Laban's younger daughter. He agreed that he would work for Laban for seven years to win Rachel as his wife. Those years "seemed to him but a few days because of the love he had for her" (29:20).

Now, however, it was Jacob who was to be tricked. Following a night of feasting, Laban gave his daughter to Jacob; but in the light of day, it was discovered that Leah, the elder daughter, had been given instead of her sister Rachel. Jacob rightly complained about the deception, only to be told that it was not proper in that country to give the younger before the firstborn.

After a week, Rachel was also given to Jacob on the condition that the bride price would be another seven years of work. So now Jacob had two wives, and the first of the two was the less loved wife. Nothing but strife could be expected in such a situation.

The advantage Leah had was that she was fertile while her sister, Rachel, was barren.

Leah bore four sons, Reuben, Simeon, Levi, and Judah; and with each birth, she hoped that Jacob would love her as he loved her sister.

Seeing that she was barren, Rachel gave her maid, Bilhah, to Jacob to bear children to her credit. (Remember the story of their grandmother, Sarah?) Bilhah bore two sons, Dan and Naphtali.

Leah decided that she too could add to her credit by giving her maid, Zilpah, to Jacob. She bore him two more sons, Gad and Asher.

Then Leah herself conceived and bore Issachar. And yet again, she bore Zebulun and then a daughter, Dinah.

Only then was Rachel able to conceive. She bore a son and named him Joseph.

Jacob continued to work for his father-in-law, Laban, in order to acquire flocks and herds. Time after time Laban changed his agreements with Jacob; nevertheless, Jacob prospered. After being with Laban for twenty years, Jacob gathered his family and possessions and set out to return to Canaan, to the land of his father, Isaac. Needless to say, Laban was not pleased, for he had thrived greatly through Jacob's efforts; and with Jacob went Laban's daughters and grandchildren. With the secret departure, Laban was now the one who was tricked.

Returning to Canaan meant a reunion with Esau; and Jacob feared that his brother, harboring hatred for what Jacob had done to him, would seek to kill him. To win Esau's favor, Jacob sent gifts of flocks and herds to him. When Esau drew near with four hundred men, Jacob feared greatly; but Esau met Jacob in peace, happily received him, and forgave him.

On the journey to Canaan, God spoke to Jacob and gave him the new name, Israel. Throughout the remainder of the Bible, these two names are used interchangeably.

In the land of Canaan, Rachel gave birth to Jacob's twelfth son, Benjamin. She died in childbirth and was buried on the way to Ephrath. This town is also known as Bethlehem, and its significance will later become abundantly clear.

For thought or discussion:

- Have you ever experienced "pay back" for a trick you have played on someone else?
- How must Leah have felt, always knowing that she was not her husband's true love?
- Is there any significance to the number 12?

12. The Bratty Kid Brother

Joseph and His Brothers
Genesis 37

Sibling rivalry is as old as Cain and Abel. It sometimes fosters healthy competition; but too often it leads to destructive pride, envy, jealousy, humiliation, anger, and hatred.

Joseph was not the youngest of Jacob's sons (Benjamin was), but his father loved him most of all because "he was the son of his old age" (37:3). Perhaps the deeper reason for such love was the fact that Joseph was the firstborn of Jacob's dearly loved wife, Rachel. Whatever the reason, Jacob's favoritism toward Joseph was clear to his brothers; and they hated him for it.

Jacob didn't help matters when he gave Joseph a coat with long sleeves. In some translations, this is described as a coat of many colors (inspiring the musical by Tim Rice and Andrew Lloyd Webber titled "Joseph and the Amazing Technicolor Dreamcoat"). The implication of a long-sleeved coat was that Joseph was important and not expected to share in all the menial tasks like mucking out stalls and washing dishes. Day by day, as he walked among his brothers, they were reminded by this coat of Joseph's special status.

Joseph didn't help matters either when he told his brothers of his dreams. He dreamed that he and his brothers were binding sheaves in the field and that his sheaf of grain stood upright while his brothers' sheaves gathered around and bowed down to his. And again, he dreamed that the sun, moon, and eleven stars were bowing down to him. While the first dream angered his brothers, the second even caused Jacob to exclaim, "What kind of dream is this that you have had? Shall we indeed come, I and your mother and your brothers, and bow to the ground before you?" (37:10). Jealousy and hatred intensified.

It happened that one day when Jacob sent Joseph to his brothers as they were tending the flock, the brothers' hatred and jealousy came to a head. Seeing him coming, wearing his famous coat, they decided that they would kill him. However, Reuben, the oldest brother, dissuaded them, urging them to put him in a pit and leave him there to die (intending to return later, to rescue him, and to restore him to their father). The other brothers stripped Joseph of his coat and threw him into a pit.

An opportunity presented itself when a caravan of Ishmaelite traders (descendants of Ishmael whom we met in story 8) passed by on their way to Egypt. Joseph's brothers pulled him out of the pit and sold him to the traders for twenty pieces of silver. So much for Joseph and his dreams of grandeur, they thought.

Reuben, returning and not knowing what his brothers had done, was greatly distressed to find that the boy was no longer in the pit. He slew a goat and dipped Joseph's robe in the blood. Then the brothers returned to Jacob with the bloody coat, and he concluded that wild animals had devoured his most loved son. Jacob grieved and was inconsolable.

For thought and discussion:

- Have you experienced sibling rivalry, and how has it shaped your life and relationships?
- Have you, either positively or negatively, experienced favoritism in school or in the workplace?
- Is there anyone to whom you show favoritism, and if so, how?

13. God Meant It for Good

Joseph in Egypt
Genesis 39-50

Joseph was taken to Egypt and sold to Potiphar, the captain of Pharaoh's guard. He had gone from favored son to slave. He had every reason to decry his fate. Nothing about this was fair.

Nevertheless, God was with Joseph, and he found favor in his master's sight. In everything that Joseph did, he prospered; and there he was given charge of all that Potiphar had. God blessed Potiphar for Joseph's sake. Joseph, it seemed, had landed on his feet.

All was well until Potiphar's wife, seeing that Joseph was a handsome man, repeatedly tried to seduce him. He continually rebuffed her advances, telling her that he would not violate Potiphar's trust and asking, "How then could I do this great wickedness, and sin against God?" (39:9). But one day when they were alone in the house, she grabbed hold of his garment, saying, "Lie with me!" Joseph fled, leaving her holding his cloak.

As the saying goes, "Hell hath no fury like a woman scorned." Potiphar's wife accused Joseph of trying to rape her, and she had his garment as evidence. Potiphar was enraged, and he put Joseph in prison. Here was yet another major setback for the once favorite son. Although he was, sadly, not the first or last innocent person to be imprisoned, imagine his despair.

God was with Joseph even in that place. He found such favor with the chief jailer that everything concerning the other prisoners was committed to Joseph's care.

Joseph had angered his brothers by sharing his dreams with them, but dealing with dreams became the path to Joseph's freedom and honor. It began with correctly interpreting the dreams of two men, the royal cupbearer, and the royal baker, who had been imprisoned for offending Pharaoh. Joseph told the cupbearer that in three days he would be restored to Pharaoh's favor and service, and he told the baker that in three days he would be executed. Both things came to pass, and Joseph asked the cupbearer to mention him to Pharaoh so that he too might be set free.

Two years later, Pharaoh dreamed two dreams that greatly troubled him. When his magicians and wise men were unable to interpret the dreams, the cupbearer finally remembered Joseph and told Pharaoh about him. Joseph was summoned, and asserting that God would give the correct interpretation, he told Pharaoh what was to be. There would be seven years of amazing abundance in Egypt, followed by seven years of severe famine. Food would need to be stored in great quantity in the years of plenty in order to survive the years of want.

As it had happened with Potiphar and the chief jailer, God caused Joseph to have such favor in Pharaoh's eyes that Joseph was put in charge of all the affairs of Egypt. Only Pharaoh himself was more powerful than Joseph. Joseph was to manage the collection and storage of food and then later to oversee its distribution.

As famine took hold of Egypt and the surrounding lands, Joseph's ten older brothers were sent by their father, Jacob, to buy grain in Egypt. Joseph recognized his brothers, but they did not recognize him. Accusing the brothers of being spies, he questioned them at length about their father and family. They told him that Jacob was well, that one brother was no more, and that their youngest brother was yet in Canaan.

Joseph imprisoned Simeon and sent the others on their way. He told them that they would need to return with Benjamin if they wanted to ransom Simeon or buy more provisions.

The famine continued, and more grain was needed by Jacob and his family. Over Jacob's strong objection, the brothers took Benjamin when they returned to Egypt. They were reunited with Simeon, and the eleven brothers came into Joseph's presence and bowed before him. The dreams of Joseph's youth had come to fruition.

Joseph revealed himself to his brothers, and he charged them to return to Canaan and to bring Jacob and the rest of the family to Egypt. With Pharaoh's blessing, Jacob and his family, a total of seventy people, settled in the area called Goshen. There they thrived even in the midst of the famine.

Sometime later, Jacob died. His sons took his body back to Canaan and buried him in the burial plot that Abraham had purchased for the family.

After Jacob's death, Joseph's brothers feared that he would now seek revenge for their cruel treatment of him. They told Joseph that Jacob had asked him to forgive them. Joseph replied, "Do not be afraid! Am I in the place of God? Even though you intended to do harm to me, God intended it for good, in order to preserve a numerous people, as he is doing today" (50:19-20).

Divine favor came to all of these people through the favorite son. Once again, this is a foreshadowing of what is to come centuries later.

For thought or discussion:

- Have you ever suffered wrongly for something you did not do?
- Have you ever caused someone else to suffer for something he or she did not do?
- Have you experienced good coming from something that did not seem good when it happened?

14. Who Am I Really?

Moses
Exodus 1 and 2

Over the course of four hundred years, the seventy Israelites (Jacob/Israel and his descendants — also referred to as Hebrews) grew to be a numerous and mighty people in Egypt. As the years passed, and as one Pharaoh after another ascended to the throne, there came a time when Joseph was at best a dusty memory and Pharaoh's love for him was long forgotten.

It often happens that when personal relationships between people of different groups or races cease, suspicions and caricatures develop and fear and hatred take hold. So it was with the Egyptians toward the Israelites. This led Pharaoh to take two actions. The first was to enslave the Israelites, using their forced labor to carry out all of the building plans and field work of the Egyptians. The second action, undertaken because the Israelites continued to multiply, was to decree that every male child born to the Israelites was to be thrown into the Nile and drowned.

Amram and Jochebed, both descendants of Levi, had a new baby boy. They kept him hidden for three months. When it was no longer possible to do so, Jochebed put her son in a papyrus basket and placed it among the reeds beside the river. Miriam, her daughter, kept watch to see what would happen.

Pharaoh's daughter came to the river to bathe. She saw the basket and sent her maid to fetch it. Seeing the infant and hearing him crying, she was moved with pity. Though she knew that this was a Hebrew child, she nevertheless decided to keep him as her son. Miriam asked if she should find a Hebrew woman to nurse the baby. When Pharaoh's daughter answered in the affirmative, Miriam brought the baby's mother who was instructed, "Take this child and nurse it for me, and I will give you your wages" (2:9).

It is certain that Jochebed did not merely nurse her son. She loved him and tended to all of his needs. She sang him lullabies and told him the stories of the LORD God and of his chosen people. She taught him that he was a descendant of Abraham, Isaac, and Jacob.

After some years, Jochebed brought him to Pharaoh's daughter, and he became her son. "She named him Moses, 'because,' she said, 'I drew him out of the water'" (2:10). In the years that followed, Moses was raised in Pharaoh's house, and learned the lore of Egypt. He was taught that he was an Egyptian, a grandson of Pharaoh.

One day, when Moses was fully grown, he went to observe the forced labor of his people. He saw an Egyptian beating one of the Israelites, and this so enraged him that he killed the Egyptian and buried him in the sand. When Pharaoh heard of it, he sought to kill Moses.

Moses fled far to the east to the land of Midian. There, having aided seven shepherdesses, he found welcome in the house of their father, Jethro, the priest of Midian. Moses was given one of the daughters, Zipporah, as a wife. Together they had two sons. Moses named the first son Gershom, "for he said, 'I have been an alien residing in a foreign land'" (2:22).

Israelite, Egyptian, resident alien in Midian — Moses was all three. Which descriptor was the essential one? How would the three strands weave together to direct his life and to shape his future?

For thought and discussion:

- Which stories of your heritage shape your life today, and how?
- Have there been times when you have been confused about who you really are?
- When people tell stories about you, how does that make you feel?

15. I Am Who I Am

Moses' Call from God
Exodus 3 and 4

One day as Moses tended his father-in-law's flock, God caught his attention in a most unusual way. Pasturing the sheep near Mount Horeb, Moses saw a bush that was on fire but was not being consumed. Nearing this bush, he was instructed to "Remove the sandals from your feet, for the place on which you are standing is holy ground" (3:5). God also said, "I have observed the misery of my people who are in Egypt; I have heard their cry on account of their taskmasters…and I have come down to deliver them" (3:7-8).

Then God announced that Moses was to be the chosen instrument to accomplish this and to lead the people to "a good and broad land, a land flowing with milk and honey" (3:8). Deliver the Israelites from slavery in Egypt and shepherd them to the land promised of old to Abraham, Isaac, and Jacob. Sounds like a dream assignment, right? This was not exactly what Moses was prepared to hear.

The first clarification Moses demanded was to know God's name, for it would be essential to know whose message he was delivering when he came to speak to the Israelites. God identified himself to Moses as, "I AM WHO I AM." God went on to say, "Thus you shall say to the Israelites, 'I AM has sent me to you'" (3:14).

What do these names mean? In the Hebrew, the first name can also mean, "I HAVE BEEN WHO I HAVE BEEN," or "I WILL BE WHO I WILL BE." The God speaking to Moses is the one who alone defines God and determines all things. The name, "I AM" (which we will hear again in amazing ways as the biblical story moves to its climax), declares that life itself and the creator of all that exists is the God who appeared to Moses. God is beyond every description that we would choose to give.

Knowing God's name did not settle things for Moses. He objected that the people in Egypt might not listen to him. God gave him signs to perform to demonstrate God's power at work. Moses countered that he was not an eloquent speaker. God reminded Moses that it was God who gives speech and has ample power to direct the speaker. Objections raised and solutions given.

This left Moses with only one plea, "O my Lord, please send someone else" (4:13). This was the last straw, but it had no power to change God's mind or plan. God did, however, say that Aaron, Moses' brother, would go with him and would be the primary one to speak to the people. The power of God was to be manifest through Moses, and Aaron was to be his spokesman.

Taking his staff, with which he was to demonstrate wondrous signs, Moses reluctantly set off to meet his brother at Mount Horeb. Together they traveled to Egypt to be God's instrument of deliverance for the people God had chosen to bring blessing to the world.

For thought and discussion:

- Have you ever believed that God wanted you to do something that you did not want to do?
- What gifts or talents has God given to you, and how do you use them to serve God and others?
- Does it frustrate you to know that God is beyond what you can fully know or define?

16. Let My People Go!

Passover and Exodus
Exodus 5-15

Rulers do not like to be told what to do. When Moses and Aaron came to Pharaoh and said, "Thus says the LORD, the God of Israel, 'Let my people go, so that they may celebrate a festival to me in the wilderness,'" (5:1) Pharaoh reacted exactly as one would expect him to react. He denied the request and then increased the heavy burden he had already placed on the backs of the Israelites. He had no intention of being deprived of his workforce and losing the prosperity they provided to him and to his nation.

To demonstrate God's power, Moses and Aaron stood before Pharaoh, and Aaron's staff was changed into a snake. Not to be outdone, the Egyptian magicians did the same thing, but Aaron's snake ate the snakes of the magicians. Pharaoh was not particularly impressed.

There followed a series of ten plagues. Moses struck the Nile with his staff, and the water turned into blood. The magicians added to this. A week later, with Pharaoh still unwilling to let the people go, Moses warned that swarms of frogs would fill the land, coming into all the houses, into beds, ovens, and kneading bowls. Pharaoh ignored the warning. Therefore, it happened. Yet again, the magicians also produced frogs. What sort of added blessing was it that the magicians could compound all the difficulties God brought on the land? Power resisted power.

The next plague was changing the dust of the land into gnats, so that gnats were everywhere. This the magicians could not do, and they told Pharaoh that "This is the finger of God!" (8:19). But once more, Pharaoh's heart was hardened.

The next six plagues fell heavily on all Egypt except for the land of Goshen where the Israelites lived. God made a distinction between his chosen people and the Egyptians. There were flies, deadly pestilence on the livestock, boils, deadly hail, locusts, and darkness that was so thick that it could be felt.

As the plagues occurred, wave after wave, Pharaoh began to relent slightly. He said that the men could go, but not the women or children. Then he said that all the people could go, but that they would need to leave their livestock behind. Time after time, Pharaoh's heart was hardened.

To prepare for the final plague, the death of the firstborn throughout Egypt, Moses spoke God's word to the Israelites. Each household was to take a year-old male lamb, without spot or blemish, on the tenth of the month; and on the fourteenth, they were to slaughter it and consume it entirely. They were to eat the meal in haste, prepared to go at a moment's notice. Prior to the meal, they were to mark the doorposts and the lintel of each house with the blood of the lamb they had slain. All the houses so marked would be passed over by the angel of death as it moved through the land. There was no distinction between Goshen and the rest of Egypt; obedience would lead to life and disobedience to death. This was the LORD's passover.

The cry of grief resounded from the king's palace to the most humble hovel, and finally Pharaoh relented. "Rise up, go away from my people, both you and the Israelites! Go, worship the LORD, as you said. Take your flocks and your herds, as you said, and be gone" (12:31-32).

The Israelites went, six hundred thousand men plus women and children. They went, having asked for (and willingly been given) objects of gold and silver from their Egyptian neighbors, thus bearing away some of the wealth of Egypt. They also carried the bones of Joseph, fulfilling the solemn oath that had been made to him when he had said, "God will surely take notice of you, and then you must carry my bones with you from here" (13:19).

God led the people in a pillar of cloud by day and a pillar of fire by night so that they could travel both day and night. They journeyed for three days and camped by the Red Sea.

Pharaoh repented of the decision he had made to allow the Israelites to leave. He set out with chariots and soldiers to reclaim his slaves. They drew near, apparently trapping the Israelites by the sea; but Moses said, "Do not be afraid, stand firm, and see the deliverance that the LORD will accomplish for you... The Lord will fight for you, and you have only to keep still" (14:13-14).

At God's command, Moses stretched out his staff, the waters of the Red Sea were divided, and the Israelites crossed on dry ground. The pillar of cloud moved between the Israelites and the Egyptians to keep them separated. When the Egyptians were again able to pursue the Israelites into the Red Sea, their chariot wheels were clogged and their progress was halted. Moses stretched out his hand, and the waters returned, drowning the Egyptians. Miriam, Moses' sister, sang: "Sing to the LORD, for he has triumphed gloriously; horse and rider he has thrown into the sea" (15:21).

These two events, the Passover and the Exodus, are climactic events; and they have forever shaped the story of the Jewish people. Each year, at the Passover Seder, the youngest child asks questions, starting with, "Why is this night different from all other nights?" The story is retold.

The Passover and Exodus are also the heritage of Christian people and a prelude to another sacrificial lamb and the deliverance from bondage to sin and death that lamb will bring.

For thought and discussion:

- Does this story of deliverance from slavery have any resonance in your life?
- From what do you yearn to be set free?
- How might God use you as an instrument to bring about the deliverance of other people?

17. Ten Words of Love

Ten Commandments
Exodus 20

Words taken out of context can easily be misunderstood. So it is with the words God spoke to his beloved people.

Three months after leaving Egypt, the people of Israel came into the wilderness of Sinai and camped in front of Mount Sinai (also known as Mount Horeb). Moses ascended the mountain and received God's instructions, testimony, and commandments. The first part of these is known as the Ten Commandments (see note at end of this story).

Commands are generally not appreciated unless it is absolutely clear that they are given for the good of the hearers and not merely to demonstrate the power of the speaker.

God began by setting the context: "I am the LORD your God, who brought you out of the land of Egypt, out of the house of slavery" (20:2). God, the giver of all things, acted in love to deliver; and He desires only the best for his beloved.

The commandments are, in essence, a because…therefore, and they are given to protect the precious gifts that God has bestowed. God is the only true God, so do not turn aside and worship other pretend gods or make images to worship. God has allowed people to know and call on God by name, so do not take that lightly or speak God's name carelessly or for evil. God has given the awesome privilege of worshiping him, so do not neglect the necessity of keeping God central to life. God has placed us in families and has given authority to parents, so do not turn away from proper guidance. God has given life itself, so do not destroy it. God has given the precious gift of marriage, so do not violate the sacred vows it entails. God has given us the things we need, so do not take what is not yours. God has given each individual his or her good name, so do not tell lies about other people. God has given us possessions, so do not seek to gain the things, spouse, or workers that belong to someone else.

These are not trivial matters. These instructions are not designed to make people jump through unnecessary hoops, nor are they given to make life difficult or joyless. These are true statements about what is necessary if people are to live together in the peace and harmony that God intends. God is simply honest, and God always tells the truth.

The punishment for disobedience is built into the commandments themselves. Consider the commandment to not tell lies. Human relationship and community are built on trust. If a person begins to tell lies, relationships will remain intact until the lies are discovered. At that point, a fracture will occur that is nearly impossible to repair. Transgressing the commandment destroys the community it was given to protect. It is like that with all of these words from God.

God said, "I the LORD your God am a jealous God, punishing children for the iniquity of parents, to the third and the fourth generation of those who reject me, but showing steadfast love to the thousandth generation of those who love me and keep my commandments" (20:5-6). While it may seem unfair for children to suffer for the sins of their parents, this too is actually the way things work in human communities. Consider for example, if parents hate people of a different race or nation, they will, through their words and actions, teach this hatred to their children. Growing up in this atmosphere of racism, the children are imbued with the same hatred; and they are likely to pass it on to their own children. The untruth of one generation becomes the truth of the next. On and on it goes. So it is also with infidelity, disregard for life, rebellion against proper authority, etc. One generation learns from another; and sin is replicated, embraced, and enhanced.

The key to all the commandments is the first one. If God is truly at the center of life and of all decisions, the rest of the commandments will naturally be followed. The sad fact is that rebellion against God, and the conviction that God's instructions are no better than human reasoning, is as old as the Garden of Eden. The tendency to ignore and violate these words of love from God, and the consequences of this ongoing rebellion, are abundantly clear every day all throughout the world.

For thought or discussion:

- Which of the Ten Commandments is the most challenging for you?
- When have you been blessed by resisting the temptation to violate one of the commandments?
- Do you see how the Ten Commandments reveal God's love for you?

Note: There are two ways of numbering the Ten Commandments:	
1. Have no other gods.	1. Have no other gods.
2. Do not misuse God's name.	2. Make no graven images.
3. Remember the sabbath day.	3. Do not misuse God's name.
4. Honor your father and mother.	4. Remember the sabbath day.
5. Do not kill.	5. Honor your father and mother.
6. Do not commit adultery.	6. Do not kill.
7. Do not steal.	7. Do not commit adultery.
8. Do not bear false witness.	8. Do not steal.
9. Do not covet neighbor's property.	9. Do not bear false witness.
10. Do not covet neighbor's wife or workers.	10. Do not covet.

18. Can God Be Trusted?

Spies Sent Into Canaan
Numbers 13 and 14

After two years, God led the people of Israel from the wilderness of Sinai to the southern border of the land of Canaan. This was the land promised as an everlasting possession to Abraham, Isaac, and Jacob.

At God's direction, Moses sent twelve men, one from each of the twelve tribes of Israel (see note at end of this chapter) to spy out the land. For forty days these men traversed the country, making note of the size of the towns, the number of inhabitants, the nature of the land itself, and the quality and quantity of its produce. They returned with their report and with samples of the produce — including a cluster of grapes that was so huge that it was carried on a pole by two men. (The logo for Israel's Ministry of Tourism today is two men carrying a cluster of grapes.)

The report of the spies was that the land was good and broad, flowing with milk and honey. That was the good news. The bad news was that the people were numerous, that the towns were large and well-fortified, and that there were giants in the land.

Ten of the twelve spies convinced the people that to inhabit Canaan was impossible. Two of the twelve, Caleb and Joshua, declared that God would give the land into the hands of the Israelites. The Israelites sided with the ten and said, "Would that we had died in the land of Egypt! Or would that we had died in this wilderness! Why is the LORD bringing us into this land to fall by the sword? Our wives and our little ones will become booty; would it not be better for us to go back to Egypt?" (14:2-3).

Why did the people doubt God? They had seen the plagues God brought against the Egyptians, and they had experienced the wonder of the exodus and the parting of the Red Sea. When they had grumbled that they would starve or die of thirst in the wilderness, God had provided manna day after day, quail beyond numbering, and water from a rock. Each day they had observed the pillars of cloud and fire. They had seen God descend upon Mount Sinai in fire, smoke, and lightning, and they had heard him speak in a voice that caused them to tremble. When they had grown tired of waiting for Moses to descend from the mountain and had made for themselves a golden calf to worship, they had experienced God's consuming wrath. They had observed Moses' shining face each time he had met with God in the tent of meeting. After the tabernacle had been completed, they had seen the cloud and the glory of God's presence descend upon it.

What further proof did they need to believe that God was powerful beyond anything else and that God could be trusted?

As it had been in Eden, once again God gave the people the consequence of their decision. God declared that the Israelites would wander in the wilderness for forty years until all of the men of that faithless generation (except for Caleb and Joshua) died. God would, in fact, give the promised land to their "little ones."

This word from the LORD was clearly not what the people wanted to hear. Therefore, the men decided to change God's mind by going up and conquering the land. This was yet another rebellion. To go when commanded was one thing. To go when forbidden was quite another. God's word is to be obeyed whether it pleases the hearers or not. To disobey is to court trouble, and trouble is easily found.

For thought or discussion:

- What experiences in your life give you reasons to trust God?
- What things in your experience cause you to distrust God?
- Can your doubts or distrust cause God's purposes to fail?

Note: The twelve tribes of Israel are essentially (but not exactly) the descendants of the twelve sons of Jacob. Jacob's sons were Reuben, Simeon, Levi, Judah, Dan, Naphtali, Gad, Asher, Issachar, Zebulun, Joseph, and Benjamin. Instead of being an inheriting tribe, the descendants of Levi became the priests of Israel. To keep the number of tribes at twelve, Joseph was replaced by his two sons, Ephraim and Manasseh.

19. The Journey's End

Into the Promised Land
Joshua

When the forty years of wilderness wandering were completed, the people of Israel prepared to enter the land that God had promised to their ancestors. The wilderness years were to have been a time in which the people learned obedience and came to rely on God. They had Moses to lead and instruct them. They repeatedly saw signs and wonders to remind them of God's power.

Moses led Israel to the edge of the land, but he was not to lead them into it. At God's direction and prior to his death, Moses passed the torch to Joshua, his protege. Moses reminded the Israelites of God's mighty acts and of the commandments and instructions that God had given. Moses charged the Israelites to worship only the LORD God and not to turn and worship the gods of the peoples of the land they were to enter. (Remember the move of Abraham and Sarah.) Moses outlined the blessings of obedience and the consequences of disobedience.

Moses was a tough act to follow. Imagine how Joshua must have felt as he took up the mantle of leadership, but God said to him, "Be strong and courageous; do not be frightened or dismayed, for the LORD your God is with you wherever you go" (1:9).

In preparation for crossing the Jordan River and entering the land of Canaan, Joshua sent two spies to scout out the city of Jericho. They entered the city and the house of a prostitute named Rahab. She hid them from the authorities who had heard that they had come. She told the spies that the people of the land, having heard of God's deliverance of Israel from Egypt and of the conquering of the kings and lands east of the Jordan, were in dread of the Israelites. She also exacted a promise from the spies that, in exchange for her assistance, she and her family would be spared when Jericho was destroyed.

In a series of events reminiscent of the exodus itself, the people of Israel crossed the Jordan River on dry ground. Though the river overflowed its banks at that time of year, when the priests carrying the ark of the covenant (the sacred box that contained the tablets of the law from Mount Sinai and a jar of manna) set foot in the water, the waters stood up in a heap and ceased to flow. The people crossed over; and twelve large stones were taken from the center of the river, one for each tribe. These were to be set up as a perpetual reminder of God's delivering power. With the Israelites safely across, the priests came up out of the riverbed, and the water resumed its flow.

Now that they were in the promised land, all of the men were circumcised as a sign of the covenant and to remind them that life itself belongs to God. The Israelites celebrated the Passover, remembering God's love and deliverance. The next day they ate of the produce of the land, and manna was no longer provided. A messenger from God told Joshua (as Moses had been told at the burning bush), "Remove the sandals from your feet, for the place where you stand is holy" (5:15).

So what was the first step in taking possession of the land? It was to conquer Jericho. This was done in a surprising way. At the LORD's direction, the armed men of Israel marched around the city following the ark of the covenant and seven priests blowing rams horns. Other than the blaring of the horns and the tramping of the feet, there was no other sound. Once around the city, and back to camp they went. They repeated this for five more days. This must have been most disconcerting for the people of Jericho. Day after day, the tension would have mounted and fear would have increased. Here was psychological warfare at its best.

On the seventh day, the Israelites marched around Jericho seven times. Then at the blast of the horns, all the soldiers shouted; and the walls of Jericho fell straight down. All of the inhabitants, except for Rahab and her family, were destroyed; and the items of silver, gold, bronze, and iron were placed in the treasury of the house of the LORD.

There followed a series of campaigns against the kings and cities throughout Canaan, and the land was settled by the Israelites. Nine and a half tribes divided up the land between the Jordan River and the Great Sea (also known as the Mediterranean). The other tribes (Reuben, Gad, and half of Manesseh) settled in the territory to the east of the Jordan River, in the land conquered under Moses' leadership.

The temptation to go against God's instructions would be constant, and so Joshua spoke to the people. "Now therefore revere the LORD and serve him in sincerity and in faithfulness; put away the gods that your ancestors served beyond the River and in Egypt, and serve the LORD. Now if you are unwilling to serve the LORD, choose this day whom you will serve, whether the gods your ancestors served in the region beyond the river or the gods of the Amorites in whose land you are living; but as for me and my household, we will serve the LORD" (24:14-15).

The resounding response of the people was "We also will serve the LORD, for he is our God" (24:18).

Promises, promises.

For thought and discussion:

- Have you ever had to succeed a powerful and well-loved leader? What were the challenges?
- Is there any place that you regard as holy ground?
- Is it easy to follow through on the promises you have made?

20. Who Says Only Men Can Have Power?

Deborah
Judges 4 and 5

How soon the wonders of God are forgotten. After Joshua and all those who had settled Canaan died, the next generation forgot the promise that their fathers and mothers had made. They turned aside and worshiped the gods of the Canaanites. Instead of remaining a people who were set apart, they intermarried with the nations among whom they lived. They forsook the LORD and worshiped Baal and other idols, so God brought upon them the consequences of disobedience; and they suffered greatly at the hands of their enemies.

Though all the Israelites had the same ancestry and the same history, they were divided into twelve independent tribes. There was no central authority, and tribes interacted according to what was deemed to be in the best interest of each tribe. The last verse of the book of Judges sums it up this way: "In those days there was no king in Israel; all the people did what was right in their own eyes" (21:25).

The Book of Judges describes the oppression that came upon the various tribes from the enemies who rose up and conquered them. When the people cried to the LORD, God would raise up a judge who would rally the people and drive out the oppressors. The judges, as military leaders, led the tribes to victory. Thereafter, having gained honor, they would decide disputes and lead the people in faithfulness to God. When the judge died, the people reverted to their evil ways.

Israel's history was an ongoing cycle of rebellion against God, punishment meted out through a neighboring nation, a cry for deliverance, victory and freedom won under the leadership of a judge, a time of peace and holiness, and back again to rebellion.

Unique among the judges was Deborah. She was a prophetess who sat as a judge in the hill country of Ephraim, and the Israelites readily came to her for judgment. She came to prominence as an arbiter of disputes rather than as a military leader.

In Deborah's time, the Israelites had been sold into the hand of King Jabin of Canaan, whose general was a man named Sisera. The Canaanites oppressed the Israelites cruelly for twenty years.

At God's direction, Deborah summoned Barak and told him to gather an army of ten thousand men from the tribes of Naphtali and Zebulun to do battle with Sisera and the Canaanite army. Barak said that he would go only if Deborah went with him. She said, "I will surely go with you; nevertheless, the road on which you are going will not lead to your glory, for the LORD will sell Sisera into the hand of a woman" (4:9).

The army of Barak routed the army of Sisera, bringing deliverance by the hand of God. Sisera himself fled on foot and sought refuge in the tent of Jael, the wife of Heber the Kenite, for there was a treaty between Heber and the Canaanites. Jael welcomed Sisera and covered him with a rug to hide him. When he requested water, she comforted him with milk, and he fell asleep. So far, it sounds like good news for the weary general.

As Sisera slept, however, Jael, taking a tent peg in one hand and a hammer in the other, drove the tent peg through his skull and killed him. Just as Deborah had foretold, Sisera's death was at the hand of a woman. When Barak came to the tent of Jael, she proudly showed him the man he had been pursuing.

Deborah and Barak sang a song that day, praising God for victory over the Canaanites. They celebrated God's raising up of Deborah and the choosing of Barak. They lauded the men who had nobly fought, and they chastised the tribes that did not rally to the cause. Lest any forget, they sang, "Most blessed of women be Jael, the wife of Heber the Kenite, of tent-dwelling women most blessed" (5:24).

And the land had rest for forty years.

For thought or discussion:

- Have you seen how evil cycles through one generation after another?
- Have you ever worked hard on a project only to have someone else receive glory for its success?
- What song might you sing to praise God for what has occurred in your life?

21. Shearing a Vow of Its Power

Samson
Judges 13-16

Othniel, Ehud, Shamgar, Deborah, Gideon, Tola, Jair, Jephthah, Ibzan, Elon, Abdon, and then there was Samson. Renowned for his incredible strength, Samson was a Nazirite from birth and the last of the judges recorded in the Book of Judges.

To understand the story of Samson, it is necessary to begin with the announcement an angel of God gave to his mother. "Behold, you are barren and have no children; but you shall conceive and bear a son. Therefore beware, and drink no wine or strong drink, and eat nothing unclean…No razor shall come upon his head, for the boy shall be a Nazirite to God from birth; and he shall begin to deliver Israel from the hand of the Philistines" (13:3-5 RSV).

A Nazirite was a sign person. Either a man or a woman could make a special vow for a particular period of time to be a Nazirite. During the time of the vow, that person was not to eat or drink anything produced by the grapevine, shave or cut his or her hair, or go near a dead body (not even of parents or siblings). As that person walked among the Israelites, she or he was to be a reminder that God was among the people.

Samson fell in love with a Philistine woman, and though his parents urged him to marry an Israelite woman instead, he was insistent. "Get her for me," he said, "because she pleases me" (14:3).

On his way to visit this woman, a young lion roared at Samson, and he slew it with his bare hands. When he passed that way later, on his way to Timnah for his marriage, he turned aside and saw that in the carcass of the lion there was a swarm of bees and honey. This led Samson, during the wedding feast, to put a riddle before thirty of the guests. If they could solve the riddle within the seven days of the feast, he would give each of them a linen garment and a festal garment. If not, they would each give him two garments. The riddle was this: "Out of the eater came something to eat. Out of the strong came something sweet" (14:14).

After wrestling unsuccessfully with the riddle for three days, the men went to Samson's wife. They threatened her. "Coax your husband to explain the riddle to us, or we will burn you and your father's house with fire" (14:15).

She begged Samson to tell her the answer to the riddle. She wept, pleaded, and nagged him until at last, on the seventh day of the feast, he told her. She in turn told the men. Before the sun set they said to Samson, "What is sweeter than honey? What is stronger than a lion?" (14:18). In anger, Samson returned to his parent's house, and his wife was given to one of the men of Timnah.

Sometime later, when he went to visit his wife and learned that she had been given to another man, he was enraged. He burned the fields and vineyards and olive groves of the Philistines. In retribution, the Philistines burned the woman and her father and then set out to capture and destroy Samson. But Samson, with the jawbone of a donkey, slew a thousand Philistines.

Samson fell in love with another Philistine woman. Her name was Delilah. The lords of the Philistines offered her a handsome sum of money to learn from Samson the source of his great strength. The plan was to lie in wait, and as soon as the secret was learned and the remedy applied, they would seize Samson and subdue him.

Delilah asked, and Samson said that if he was bound with seven fresh bowstrings, he would become weak. She bound him with the bowstrings, the Philistines rushed at him, and he snapped the bowstrings and defeated his would-be captors.

Delilah asked again, and he said that if he was bound with new ropes that had never been used, he would be weak like any other man. She bound him, the Philistines attacked, he snapped the ropes and again prevailed.

Delilah pouted and chastised him for mocking her and telling her lies. She asked again for the secret of his strength. Samson told her that if the seven locks of his hair were woven into a web and fastened with a pin, he would lose his strength. She did it, they attacked, Samson shook loose his hair, and he overcame his attackers.

This should have been three strikes and you're out, but Samson was a slow learner.

Delilah nagged him day after day (*if you really loved me...*) until he finally told her that his strength was in his hair and in the Nazirite vow which it represented. While he slept with his head on her lap, she had his hair shorn. When the Philistines rushed in, he was powerless to defend himself. The vow was broken, and Samson's power was gone.

The Philistines gouged out his eyes, bound him with bronze shackles, and set him to work grinding at the mill in their prison. Samson's hair began to grow back.

There came a time when the Philistines held a great festival for their god Dagon, and thousands filled the building to celebrate. They sent for Samson so that he could entertain them as they rejoiced in their victory over him. Placing his hands on the chief pillars of the building, and asking God for one last feat of strength, he brought down the house, killing all who were in it. Ironically, Samson killed more people in his death than in his life.

For thought or discussion:

- Have you found it difficult to live up to the expectations others have for you?
- Have you ever been slow or unwilling to learn from your mistakes?

22. Your People Shall Be My People

Naomi and Ruth
Ruth

During the time of the judges, and when there was a famine in the land, Elimelech and Naomi, with their sons Mahlon and Chilion, moved from Bethlehem in Judah to the country of Moab. During the decade they lived there, Elimelech died, the boys married Moabite women, and the boys died. This left Naomi with two daughters-in-law, Orpah and Ruth.

Hearing that the famine had ended, Naomi decided to return to Judah so that she could live out her life among her own people. Her daughters-in-law set out with her, but she urged them to return to their mothers' homes and find new husbands from among the Moabites. It made perfect sense, and it was the logical thing for the two young women to do.

Orpah turned back, but Ruth did not. Instead, she said, "Entreat me not to leave you or to return from following you; for where you go I will go, and where you lodge I will lodge; your people shall be my people, and your God my God" (1:16 RSV). Naomi and Ruth traveled on together.

Arriving in Bethlehem, the two women had a place to live on the parcel of land that had belonged to Elimelech, but they had not much else. To provide food, Ruth went out each day to glean behind the reapers as the barley was being harvested. The field to which she went belonged to Boaz, a prominent wealthy kinsman of Elimelech.

When Boaz saw Ruth gleaning, he spoke kindly to her. He encouraged her to glean only in his fields and among his workers and other gleaning women. He told her that he had ordered the young men not to bother her; for then as now, a single woman, especially a foreigner, could easily be mistreated, insulted, or abused. Boaz also invited Ruth to drink of the water his workers had drawn.

Ruth prostrated herself before Boaz and asked why she had found favor in his sight. He responded, "All that you have done for your mother-in-law since the death of your husband has been fully told me…May you have a full reward from the LORD, the

God of Israel, under whose wings you have come for refuge!" (2:11-12).

At the end of the day, Ruth returned to Naomi with the barley she had gleaned. Naomi was impressed with the amount Ruth had gleaned and inquired as to the events of the day and the details of her labor. Naomi was pleased to hear that it was in the field of Boaz that Ruth had labored, and she encouraged her to glean only in his fields. All through the barley and wheat harvests, this is what Ruth did.

Naomi had something else in mind as well. She told Ruth that she was concerned about security for her daughter-in-law, and so she outlined a plan to provide it. Knowing that Boaz would be threshing barley that night, and that he would sleep in the field, she told Ruth to wash, anoint herself, put on her best clothes, notice where Boaz slept, and go and lie down at his feet.

Ruth did as instructed. Seeing where Boaz slept, she uncovered his feet and lay down there. When Boaz awoke with a start and found a woman lying at his feet, he asked who she was. She responded, "I am Ruth, your servant; spread your cloak over your servant, for you are next-of-kin" (3:9). On first meeting Ruth, Boaz had wished her the LORD's protection "under whose wings you have come for refuge." Now she asked him to be that protection, spreading his cloak or his wings over her. Boaz agreed to do it.

The only potential hitch in the plan was that there was one man who was a nearer kin to Elimelech, and it was his right to redeem the land if he chose to do so. The next day, Boaz met that man in the gate of Bethlehem (where the elders of the city often sat); and with witnesses, he asked the man if he wished to redeem Elimelech's land. The man said that he would. Boaz pointed out that in redeeming the land, he would also acquire Ruth, the Moabite, and that it would be up to him to raise up a child to keep Mahlon's name and inheritance alive. At this, the man declined and passed to Boaz the right of redemption.

So Ruth became the wife of Boaz. She conceived and bore a son, and they named him Obed. The women of the neighborhood said, "A son has been born to Naomi" (4:17). Naomi had suffered the death of her husband and her sons, and her life had become bitter. Now she had a loving daughter-in-law, a fine son-in-law, and a beautiful grandson; and her life was pleasant indeed.

Obed would become the father of Jesse and the grandfather of David. That is a story yet to be told.

For thought or discussion:

- What do you think motivated Ruth to cast her lot with Naomi rather than returning to Moab?
- Have you had the experience of making a similar life-changing attachment to another person?
- Ruth was treated with kindness. Is that usually how immigrants are treated?

23. A Voice in the Night

Samuel
1 Samuel 1-3

A man named Elkanah married two women, Hannah and Peninnah; and strife was rampant. The fact that Peninnah bore many children and Hannah bore none exacerbated the problem. This is all reminiscent of Jacob and his wives, Leah and Rachel.

Each year, when Elkanah and his family went up to Shiloh to worship and sacrifice to God, he gave portions to Peninnah and to her children and a double portion to Hannah, because he loved her. Peninnah provoked and irritated Hannah mercilessly, delighting to rub salt into the wound of Hannah's barrenness.

Elkanah tried to console Hannah, saying to her, "Am I not more to you than ten sons?" (1:8). Of course the answer was a resounding "No!" He meant well, but he clearly did not understand.

One year in Shiloh, Hannah, greatly distressed, prayed earnestly and promised that if God would give her a son, she would dedicate him to the LORD as a Nazirite. She prayed silently, but she moved her mouth as she prayed so that the priest, Eli, observing her, thought that she was drunk. He chastised her for making a drunken spectacle of herself. But when Hannah responded that she was not drunk but was pouring out her soul before God, Eli said, "Go in peace; the God of Israel grant the petition you have made to him" (1:17).

Hannah conceived and bore a son. She named him Samuel.

When Elkanah and his household went again to Shiloh to offer the yearly sacrifice to the LORD, Hannah stayed at home. She said that as soon as Samuel was weaned, "I will bring him, that he may appear in the presence of the LORD, and remain there for ever" (1:22).

So it was that when Samuel was weaned (two or three years old), Hannah took Samuel to Shiloh and gave him to Eli. Whether Eli, an elderly priest, was pleased with this is debatable; that Hannah was fulfilling the vow she had made to God was not. Imagine how difficult it must have been for Hannah to keep that vow and leave her little one with Eli. (By the grace of God,

Hannah later bore three sons and two daughters, but she did not know that this would be the case when she fulfilled her vow.)

Samuel grew up serving in the temple under Eli's guidance, increasing in favor with God and with all the people.

One night, as Samuel slept in the temple, the LORD called, "Samuel! Samuel!" (3:4). Samuel ran to Eli to see what he wanted. Eli said that he had not called Samuel and told him to go lie down again. Twice more this happened, and the third time Eli realized that, though God had never spoken to him, God was calling the boy. "Go, lie down; and if he calls you, you shall say, 'Speak, LORD, for your servant is listening'" (3:9).

So it happened. The LORD spoke to Samuel, revealing that he was going to punish Eli and his two sons, Hophni and Phinehas, who served as priests with their father. The sons were wicked and ungodly men. They took advantage of their position as priests to take for themselves the best portions of the sacrifices and to have sex with the women who served at the temple. They were the talk of the town. Eli rebuked them, but he did not restrain them.

When morning came, Eli inquired of Samuel what God had said to him. Samuel was understandably reluctant to be the bearer of dismal news. Eli urged Samuel to hold nothing back, and so Samuel hid nothing from Eli.

The word that God had spoken came to pass. In a battle with the Philistines, Israel was routed, Hophni and Phinehas were killed, and the ark of the covenant was captured. Eli (ninety-eight years old, nearly blind, and overweight) was sitting in a chair beside the road in Shiloh, waiting for word from the battlefield. When he received this dire news, he fell over backward in his chair, broke his neck, and died. The house of Eli had come to an end.

Samuel, on the other hand, grew strong in the LORD; and all Israel came to know that Samuel was a trustworthy prophet of God. The LORD continually revealed himself to Samuel at Shiloh; and Samuel served God faithfully as prophet, priest, and judge. Samuel was held in high esteem by the people. Each year he went on a circuit to Bethel, Gilgal, Mizpah, and Ramah to administer justice for all of Israel.

For thought or discussion:

- Both Samson and Samuel were Nazirites. How were they alike, and how were they different?
- Have you ever made a promise that was costly to fulfill?
- Have you ever had to be the bearer of bad news to someone else? How did you handle it?

24. Who Should Be King?

Samuel and Saul
1 Samuel 8-11

When Samuel grew old, he appointed his sons to carry on the work that he had done. Unfortunately, as is all too often the case, the boys were not like their father. They were not honorable and godly men. They were greedy for gain, took bribes, and perverted justice. They did not walk in the way of the LORD as their father had always done.

Therefore, the elders of Israel came to Samuel and said, "You are old and your sons do not follow in your ways; appoint for us, then, a king to govern us, like other nations" (8:5).

This displeased Samuel, for Israel was not to be like the other nations. God was Israel's king, and the request for a human king was yet another act of rebellion. God, of course, was not surprised by such shenanigans, but he instructed Samuel to warn the people what it would mean for them to have a human king.

A king would conscript the young men to serve in his army and to make all the things related to war. A king would take the young women to be his cooks, bakers, and perfumers. He would take the choicest of the fields, vineyards and orchards for himself and the choicest of the produce that remained for his chosen leaders. He would take the best of the flocks and herds. The people would become his slaves.

The people paid little attention to what Samuel said. They declared: "No! but we are determined to have a king over us, so that we also may be like other nations, and that our king may govern us and go out before us and fight our battles." (8:19-20)

There was in the tribe of Benjamin a young man named Saul, the son of Kish. Saul was tall, dark, and handsome.

Saul's father's donkeys had wandered away, so Kish sent Saul, along with one of the servants to find the donkeys. For three days they searched far and wide with no success. The servant boy suggested that they consult the man of God (also known as the prophet or seer) who was in the nearby town. This is how they came to meet Samuel.

God had revealed to Samuel that the man who was to be anointed king would come to him that day. Samuel assured Saul that his father's donkeys were safe at home, and then he invited Saul and the boy to join him at the shrine to which he had come to bless the sacrifice and to join in the feast.

The next day, before sending Saul on his way home, Samuel poured a vial of oil on Saul's head. "The LORD has anointed you ruler over his people Israel," (10:1) he said. He also told Saul of three things that would occur as he traveled home — signs of the truth of Samuel's words. All three signs were fulfilled as promised.

Samuel then summoned the people of Israel to Mizpah. He directed the people to present themselves by tribes and by clans. By lot, the tribe of Benjamin was chosen, and then the family of the Matrites, and then Saul, son of Kish. When they looked for Saul, however, they could not find him until they discovered him hiding among the baggage.

Setting Saul in the midst of the people, Samuel declared: "'Do you see the one whom the LORD has chosen? There is no one like him among all the people.' And all the people shouted, 'Long live the king!'" (10:24)

So how did Saul deal with the first test of his kingship?

Nahash, king of the Ammonites had been oppressing the people of the tribes of Gad and Reuben. He gouged out the right eye of each person except for seven thousand men who had escaped to Jabesh-gilead. Nahash besieged that town and said he would only make peace with the people on the condition that he could also gouge out their right eyes. Not being excited at that prospect, the elders of Jabesh asked for seven days in which to seek for someone to save them. Nahash haughtily granted the delay.

When Saul learned of this, the Spirit of God came powerfully upon him. He called out the people from all the tribes of Israel and mustered a force of 370,000 men. With this army, Saul routed the Ammonites and delivered the people of Jabesh-gilead.

Samuel, Saul, and the people went to Gilgal, and there they renewed the kingship. Sacrifices were offered, and Saul and the people rejoiced greatly. Israel was no longer a confederation of tribes but a kingdom with an earthly king.

Saul aced his first test. What would the future bring for Israel and her king?

For thought or discussion:

- Is it easier for you to put your trust in God or in earthly leaders? Why?
- What do you want or expect from those who are the leaders in your country?
- What costs are you willing to pay to support those who provide political leadership?

25. The Bigger They Are...

David and Goliath
1 Samuel 17

War is a messy and horrible business. Armies mass against each other. Battles take place, and lives (especially of young men and women) are lost. The pageantry before battle may well be grand, but the battle itself is brutal. As centuries have passed, war has become somewhat less personal since newer weapons allow us to kill each other without having to fight hand to hand.

It would be so much easier and less bloody if each side would choose a representative to arm wrestle. The one who pinned the other would be the victor, and the other side would agree that it had been defeated and would accept the will of the winners.

That sounds pretty weird, doesn't it? It is a tamer version of the story of David and Goliath.

During the time of King Saul, the Philistines were the principal troublers of Israel. Gathering their armies for battle, the Philistines drew up their battle lines on one side of the valley of Elah, and the Israelite armies lined up on the other side of the valley. Everything was in readiness for a fight to the finish.

But then, from the camp of the Philistines strode forth Goliath of Gath. He was a giant, nine feet six inches in height. He challenged the Israelites to choose a champion of their own to fight against him. "Today I defy the ranks of Israel! Give me a man, that we may fight together" (17:10). Goliath said that if he could be bested, the Philistines would be Israel's slaves; but if he won, Israel would serve Philistia.

Day after day, morning and evening, Goliath stepped forward and issued his challenge, and the soldiers of Israel trembled. Actually going into battle would have been costly, but enduring this repeated challenge from Goliath must have been psychologically draining and dispiriting.

Enter David from Bethlehem. David (a great-grandson of Ruth) was the youngest of Jesse's eight sons. His three oldest brothers were with Saul's army while David tended his father's flocks.

One day, Jesse sent David with provisions for his brothers in the army. When David came to the camp, he heard Goliath's taunting challenge. Some soldiers were saying, "The king will greatly enrich the man who kills him and will give him his daughter and make his family free in Israel" (17:25). David asked, "Who is this uncircumcised Philistine that he should defy the armies of the living God?" (17:26). His brothers were irritated, but David's bravado was brought to Saul's attention.

When Saul saw that David was but a boy, he told David that he would have no chance against Goliath, who had been a warrior from youth. David, however, responded that he had slain both lion and bear when they took lambs from his flock. "The Lord, who saved me from the paw of the lion and from the paw of the bear, will save me from the hand of this Philistine" (17:37).

Saul was convinced and clothed David in his armor. Unused to armor, David could hardly move, so he removed the armor. Instead, he took his staff, put five smooth stones in his shepherd's bag, took his sling in his hand, and went out to meet Goliath.

Goliath, amused at the challenge from this ruddy youth, thundered, "Am I a dog, that you come to me with sticks?" (17:43). He cursed David and declared that he would give David's flesh to the birds of the air and to the wild animals.

David said, "You come to me with sword and spear and javelin; but I come to you in the name of the Lord of hosts, the God of the armies of Israel, whom you have defied. This very day the Lord will deliver you into my hand...so that all the earth may know that there is a God in Israel" (17:45-46).

Goliath advanced, confident of victory. David also came forward, fit a stone in his sling, and let it fly, striking Goliath in the forehead. The giant fell face down on the ground. David took Goliath's sword; and with it, he cut off Goliath's head. The Philistines, ignoring the terms of the "fight of champions" (that they would now be Israel's slaves), fled in terror, pursued by the army of Saul.

The prizes of victory for David were Goliath's sword and armor, the admiration of King Saul, and the gratitude of the people of Israel.

For thought or discussion:

- Have you ever been faced with what seemed like an insurmountable obstacle?
- What do you think of the Israelites trusting their future to the boy David?
- What is the greatest victory you have won?

26. Pride Goes Before the Fall

Saul and David
1 Samuel

Being in charge is not easy, for with the honor comes great responsibility. One aspect of leadership is knowing when to speak or act and when to refrain from doing so. Another part of the challenge is knowing to whom one is answerable.

Saul was not one who sought the kingship (as witnessed by his hiding among the baggage when he was announced as king), but he was God's anointed. As is always true, the fact that God chooses a person does not mean that the chosen one becomes a marionette, dancing on the strings that God pulls. God makes known the purpose of the choosing, and the one chosen decides day by day whether to follow or to turn aside, whether to earnestly seek to do God's will or to seek personal glory and power.

It didn't take long for Saul to begin to stray. The first instance was when the Philistines advanced against Israel (chapter 13). Saul and his men were in Gilgal, waiting for Samuel to come and offer the appropriate sacrifices prior to engaging in battle. Samuel had said that he would arrive in seven days; but when he was delayed, Saul became anxious. He took it upon himself, though he was not entitled to do so, to offer the sacrifices.

No sooner had Saul offered the sacrifices than Samuel arrived. (Isn't that how it always is when we do things that are not ours to do?) Caught in the act, Saul tried to excuse his behavior as necessary to keep his men from leaving and to entreat the Lord's favor before meeting the Philistine threat. He said, "So I forced myself, and offered the burnt offering" (13:12). Samuel would have none of it; and he declared that because of Saul's disobedience, God would not permit Saul's kingdom to last but would select a new king, "a man after his own heart" (13:14).

David was the man God chose to replace Saul. Samuel, at God's direction, anointed David to succeed Saul, but until Saul's death, David was, in effect, a king in waiting.

Much to Saul's delight, David slew Goliath. Therefore, Saul was pleased to send David out to fight the enemies of Israel.

Because of David's success, Saul made him the head of his army. Every king needs a great general.

All was well until the people began to sing, "Saul has killed his thousands, and David his ten thousands" (18:7). Needless to say, Saul was very displeased, angry, and jealous. Saul's pride was sorely wounded; and from that time on, Saul was against David.

Twice (chapter 18), Saul threw a spear at David as David played his lyre and sang for Saul. This was not because David played or sang badly, but because Saul clearly sensed that "the LORD was with [David] but had departed from Saul" (18:12). David fled from Saul's presence and, with his band of men, sought refuge in the wilderness.

A number of times, Saul gathered his warriors and pursued David to kill him; and twice David had perfect opportunities to kill Saul. The first was when David and his men were hiding deep in a cave, and Saul came into the cave to relieve himself. David cut off the corner of Saul's robe but did not harm Saul. At a later time, David and one of his men came into Saul's camp while all were asleep and took Saul's spear and water bottle from beside Saul. Both times, David called out to Saul to let him know how easily he could have killed the king. But, he said, "The LORD forbid that I should do this thing to my lord…to raise my hand against him; for he is the LORD's anointed" (24:6).

David's integrity was shown in his unwillingness to usurp the throne as long as Saul lived. Saul, on the other hand, was obsessed with jealousy toward and hatred of David. Instead of seeking to do the will of God, Saul focused his time and energy on erasing David.

Repeatedly, Saul had been shown that David was a willing and loyal follower, but forever it rang in his ears, "Saul has killed his thousands, and David his ten thousands." It drove him mad!

When the Philistines came against Israel yet again, things went very badly for Saul and his army. His three sons, Jonathan, Abinadab, and Malchishua, were killed in battle; and Saul was badly wounded. Rather than risk falling into the hands of the Philistines, Saul asked his armor bearer to kill him. When the armor bearer refused, Saul fell on his own sword and died.

What could have been a long and blessed reign ran aground on the rocks of pride, jealousy, and disobedience. How the mighty had fallen!

For thought or discussion:

- Is there someone you have envied to the point of distraction?
- How have you shown loyalty to your family, friends, and those for whom you work?
- When you have been in a position of leadership, what has been your guiding principle?

27. In the Spring of the Year

David and Bathsheba
2 Samuel 11 and 12

David was a man after God's own heart.

When Samuel was instructed to anoint one of Jesse's sons to be king instead of Saul, Samuel traveled to Bethlehem to do so. Jesse had eight sons. When Samuel saw the oldest, Eliab, he assumed that he was God's chosen one. "But the LORD said to Samuel, 'Do not look on his appearance or on the height of his stature, because I have rejected him; for the LORD does not see as mortals see; they look on the outward appearance, but the LORD looks on the heart'" (1 Samuel 16:7). And so it was that David, the youngest son of Jesse, was God's choice to be king.

We know of David's stunning victory over Goliath, of the success he had in battle, and of his loyalty to Saul. David made Jerusalem his capital and brought the ark of the covenant into the city. David declared his intention to build a house for God, but the LORD told him that such a house would be built not by David but by his son. The LORD also declared to David that he would establish David's house forever.

David truly was a man after God's own heart. That does not mean that David was perfect. In fact, he was far from it.

2 Samuel, chapter 11, begins with these words: "In the spring of the year, the time when kings go out to battle…" Indeed, David sent his army to do battle with the Ammonites, but he remained in Jerusalem. It would have been better if he had gone with the army.

One afternoon, as David walked on the roof of his house, he saw a beautiful woman bathing. Her name was Bathsheba, and she was purifying herself after her period. Why she was naked in a place where it was possible to be seen — at least by a king standing on his rooftop — is unclear. That David was aroused is certain.

David, knowing full well that she was the wife of Uriah the Hittite, sent a messenger to bring her to him, and he had intercourse with her. Whether or not Bathsheba came willingly to David, it is unfortunately not the last time that a man of power (and he was the most powerful man in Israel) took advantage of a beautiful woman. Bathsheba became pregnant.

Wanting to cover his tracks, David sent for Bathsheba's husband who was with the army. At David's command, Uriah came back to Jerusalem. David acted as though his only interest was to ascertain how things were going with the campaign. Having received a report from Uriah, he encouraged him to spend the night with his wife before returning to the army. But Uriah, thinking it wrong to enjoy Bathsheba's company while his comrades were in the field, slept with David's servants. David was incredulous when he learned of this, and he urged Uriah to remain yet another night. David invited Uriah to eat and drink with him, certain that when Uriah was drunk, he would go to his wife. However, Uriah did not go down to his house and have sex with his wife.

David then added sin to sin. Seeing that Uriah would not provide the cover he needed, David sent Uriah back to the army with a letter to the commander, Joab. David directed Joab to position Uriah where the fighting would be the fiercest and then to draw back from him so that Uriah would be killed in battle. Joab did as commanded, and Uriah was slain.

News of Uriah's death was conveyed to David. Mission accomplished.

"When the wife of Uriah heard that her husband was dead, she made lamentation for him. When the mourning was over, David sent and brought her to his house, and she became his wife, and bore him a son" (11:26-27).

All's well that ends well. However, this was not the end.

God sent the prophet Nathan to David to tell him about two men, one rich and the other poor. The rich man had large flocks. The poor man had only one little ewe lamb that he cherished. A traveler came to the home of the rich man, and, instead of taking a lamb from his expansive flock, he took the poor man's one lamb and served it to his guest.

David was incensed, declaring that such a man deserved to die. Nathan said, "You are the man!" (12:7). The word from God that Nathan spoke to David was, "Now therefore the sword shall never depart from your house…I will raise up trouble against you from within your own house" (12:10-11).

David confessed, "I have sinned against the Lord," (12:13) and Nathan assured David that God had forgiven him. "Nevertheless, because by this deed you have utterly scorned the Lord, the child that is born to you shall die" (12:14). Sin always has consequences.

David *was* a man after God's own heart. Imperfect though he clearly was, he always turned back to God and accepted the Lord's correction. The highs and lows of his life are recorded in the Psalms he wrote. He rejoiced in God's love and favor. He repented of his sins. He was Israel's greatest king, reigning for forty years, and he was the one by whom all future kings would be measured. From David's lineage the promised Messiah was to come.

For thought or discussion:

- Have you ever abused power or been the victim of such abuse?
- Does it surprise you that God condemns sin and yet loves the sinner?
- Does it encourage you to know that Israel's greatest king was imperfect and yet loved by God?

28. The Wise and Magnificent Ruler

Solomon, Part 1

1 Kings 3-10

God has a strange way of bringing his good purposes to fruition through the very people who failed the test of perfect obedience. David and Bathsheba lost the son of their adultery; but it was through their second son, Solomon, that God carried on the promise.

Solomon, like David, was not his father's oldest son; but he was the one chosen to succeed his father as Israel's king. Solomon was anointed at David's direction following earlier deaths of his sons Amnon and Absalom and an attempted coup by his son Adonijah. True to Nathan's prophecy following David's adultery with Bathsheba and the arranged death of Uriah, David's household had surely been marked by trouble.

When Solomon began to reign, he walked in the way of his father. The LORD appeared to him in a dream and asked Solomon what gift he desired to have. Solomon responded, "Give your servant therefore an understanding mind to govern your people, able to discern between good and evil; for who can govern this your great people?" (3:9).

It pleased God that Solomon asked for wisdom instead of for long life, riches, or the life of his enemies. God declared, "Indeed I give you a wise and discerning mind; no one like you has been before you and no one like you shall arise after you" (3:12). God also said that he would give Solomon riches and honor so that no other king would compare with him. If Solomon would be faithful as David had been, God would also give him long life.

Solomon's wisdom and understanding were unsurpassed.

On one occasion, two women came to Solomon to have him arbitrate a dispute. The women lived in the same house, and three days apart they each bore a son. In the middle of the night, one woman accidentally lay on her child and suffocated him. Each claimed that the living baby was hers and that the dead baby belonged to the other. Solomon had a ready answer. He asked for a sword and said that he would divide the living baby in half so that the women could share him. One woman immediately begged Solomon to let the child live and asked him to give the baby to the other woman. The second woman said to divide the child in half — share and share alike. Clearly the mother of the child was the one who begged for his life. Solomon ruled in her favor.

Solomon's wisdom became legendary, and his fame spread throughout the surrounding nations. He composed three thousand proverbs and more than a thousand songs. When he was asked to answer questions about virtually any subject or to make complex decisions of state, Solomon excelled. People came from far and wide to hear the wisdom of Solomon. Notable among the visitors was the Queen of Sheba, who was dazzled by all that she saw and heard.

Solomon built the house of the LORD, the temple in Jerusalem. With the aid of artisans from King Hiram of Tyre, the temple was under construction for seven years. It was magnificent, built of quarried stone and lined with cedar from Lebanon. The cedar was carved with cherubim, palm trees, and flowers. The inner sanctuary, where the ark of the covenant was to be placed, was constructed of cedar; and all the furnishings and utensils were crafted. Most surfaces were overlaid with pure gold.

At the time of the dedication, when all things were finished and in place, Solomon gave a speech to the people and offered a prayer of dedication. Solomon acknowledged that "Even heaven and the highest heaven cannot contain you, much less this house that I have built!" (8:27). Nevertheless, knowing that the temple had been built at the LORD's direction, he prayed that whenever an individual Israelite, or all the people, or a foreigner sinned and turned toward the temple and prayed; God would forgive. Solomon then sacrificed twenty-two thousand oxen and one hundred twenty thousand sheep. The festival of dedication lasted for seven days.

Solomon had great wealth: gold, jewels, silver, and bronze almost beyond counting. "All King Solomon's drinking vessels were of gold...none were of silver—it was not considered as anything in the days of Solomon"(10:21). He had chariots and horses aplenty, immense flocks and herds, exotic animals and fowl. He had a massive ivory throne, overlaid with the finest gold.

The land that Solomon ruled had been conquered and passed on to him by David; but he essentially gilded it all.

God appeared again to Solomon in a dream and told him that his prayers had been heard. Regarding the temple, God said, "I have consecrated this house that you have built and put my name there forever; my eyes and my heart will be there for all time"(9:3). God then reiterated the promise that if Solomon would remain faithful to God, he would never lack a descendant to sit on the throne. But, God warned, if Solomon turned aside, Israel would be cut off and the temple would become a heap of ruins.

It is worth noting that while it took seven years to build the house of the LORD, Solomon spent thirteen years building his own house. Also, unlike David who expanded Israel's boundaries to their fullest extent, Solomon gave away twenty cities to King Hiram of Tyre. Giving away land was never pleasing to the people.

For thought or discussion:

- If you could ask God for one thing, what would it be?
- What is wisdom, and why is having it important?
- Who do you consider to be the wisest person you know or have known?

29. A Thousand Women to Please

Solomon, Part 2
1 Kings 11

Solomon was the wisest man who ever lived. His marriages might call this into question. "Among his wives were seven hundred princesses and three hundred concubines; and his wives turned away his heart" (11:3).

God's intent was revealed in Genesis 2:24: "Therefore a man leaves his father and his mother and clings to his wife, and they become one flesh." In story after story, as men had multiple wives, strife was constant. How can a man be one flesh, with the deepest and most complete intimacy, with more than one wife? What about trying to be one flesh with a thousand women?

Surely many of Solomon's marriages were made for political purposes, cementing pacts with the rulers of surrounding nations. Yet it is hard to imagine that all those women were content to be ignored by Solomon. Even if he was the most virile man who ever lived, how would he sexually satisfy a thousand women? How much time did he even spend with each of the women on any regular basis? While the women likely lived in luxury, don't you suppose that competition and jealousy were rampant, for each was used to being considered special.

"It's complicated" hardly begins to describe the problems that came with having a thousand women to please. The logistics alone boggles the mind, but that is but the tip of the iceberg. The greater issue was that those women turned Solomon's heart away from God.

Solomon's wives were from foreign nations concerning which God had instructed the Israelites, "You shall not enter into marriage with them, neither shall they with you; for they will surely incline your heart to follow their gods" (11:2). Solomon was drawn into the worship of the gods of his wives. He built high places for Chemosh, Molech, Astarte, Milcom, Baal, and the host of other gods his wives revered. The adage, "happy wife, happy life," played out in spades as Solomon sought to please a thousand women.

God was angry with Solomon because of his idolatry. "Since this has been your mind and you have not kept my covenant and my statutes that I have commanded you, I will surely tear the kingdom from you and give it to your servant. Yet for the sake of your father David, I will not do it in your lifetime; I will tear it out of the hand of your son. I will not, however, tear away the entire kingdom; I will give one tribe to your son, for the sake of my servant David and for the sake of Jerusalem, which I have chosen" (11:11-13).

What God required was that the king should, above all else, seek to please the LORD. When pleasing wives took precedence over pleasing God, Solomon fell from God's favor. This was the beginning of the descent down the slippery slope.

The ten northern tribes were indeed taken from Solomon's haughty son, Rehoboam, and given to a man named Jeroboam. The prophet Ahijah had foretold this to Jeroboam and had accompanied the promise with God's word that Jeroboam's house would endure as long as he was faithful to God.

Once the ten northern tribes (known hereafter as Israel) rebelled against King Rehoboam and made Jeroboam their king, Jeroboam turned the people away from the LORD. Jeroboam feared that Israel would be drawn back into the influence of King Rehoboam as the people made their pilgrimages to the house of the LORD in Jerusalem. Therefore, he made two golden calves (shades of the idolatry at Mount Sinai). He placed one golden calf at Bethel in the south and one at Dan in the north, and the people worshiped at those sites.

David reigned over a united kingdom for 33 years, and Solomon reigned for forty years. The kingdom of Israel had nineteen kings after Solomon; and not one of them walked in the ways of King David, wholeheartedly following the LORD. In 721 BC, Israel was conquered by the Assyrians. As was their practice, the Assyrians scattered the people of Israel throughout their empire and resettled the land of Israel with other peoples that they had conquered. Israel ceased to exist as a nation. This will have special relevance later in our story.

The kingdom of Judah (the southern kingdom, the tribes of Judah and Benjamin) endured for 135 years longer until it was conquered by the Babylonians in 586 BC. Of the nineteen kings and one queen who ruled Judah, five were faithful to God, walking in the ways of King David; and three others were at least partly faithful. The Babylonians, instead of scattering the people as the Assyrians had done with Israel, deported the most learned and gifted of the people *en masse* to Babylon. They left the poorest of the people in Judah to maintain the land. Judah remained a nation even in captivity.

Solomon's wives turned his heart away from the Lord, and so the wisest man proved to be less than wise. Those who came after him were led astray by their kings, by the people of the surrounding nations, and by the idols they worshiped. Hearts focused on anything other than the Lord led to dire consequences.

For thought or discussion:

- Who or what has the most influence on you today?
- Why is it so difficult to learn from history the lessons it can teach us?
- What threatens to turn your heart away from the Lord?

30. The Mountaintop and the Valley of Despair
Elijah
1 Kings 18 and 19

Throughout history, God spoke to the kings or the nation through the prophets. Their primary message was that since the people had turned from following God and had gone after idols, punishment would be meted out by God. Though the prophets also spoke of restoration and deliverance, they were not generally good dinner guests, as they usually brought dire news.

One such prophet was Elijah, who spoke to the northern kingdom during the reign of King Ahab. "Ahab did more to provoke the anger of the Lord, the God of Israel, than had all the kings of Israel who were before him" (16:33). He married Jezebel, a right wicked woman, and together they worshiped and served Baal. As the queen's name has become a pejorative description for a morally corrupt woman, so Ahab's reign stands as the epitome of wickedness.

Elijah, at God's direction, told Ahab that there would be a prolonged, severe drought in Israel. Three years into the drought, the two men met face to face; and Ahab addressed Elijah as "'you troubler of Israel.' [Elijah] answered, 'I have not troubled Israel; but you have…because you have forsaken the commandments of the Lord and followed the Baals. Now therefore have all Israel assemble for me at Mount Carmel, with the 450 prophets of Baal…who eat at Jezebel's table'" (18:17-19).

The contest on Mount Carmel was to demonstrate whether Baal or the Lord was really God. The prophets of Baal were to build an altar, cut up a bull and lay it on the altar, and then call on Baal to ignite the fire. Elijah would do the same, calling on the Lord.

The prophets of Baal, all 450 of them, danced around the altar calling on Baal. For hours they limped around the altar, crying aloud and cutting themselves as they waited on Baal. Elijah mocked them, suggesting that Baal must be meditating, relieving himself, sleeping, or away on a journey. No lightning bolt lit their fire.

When it was Elijah's turn, he prepared the altar with twelve stones (one for each tribe), placed the wood and the bull on the altar, and had water poured over it three times until it filled the trench around the altar. Then he called on the LORD. Fire came from heaven and consumed the bull, the wood, the altar, and even the water in the trench. Elijah then directed that the prophets of Baal should all be killed, and it was done.

As a further sign of God's power, Elijah told Ahab that as he drove his chariot to Jezreel, the rain would come and end the drought. And so it happened. The powerlessness of Baal was demonstrated; the power of the LORD was made manifest. Elijah had won a wondrous victory.

Jezebel was not amused. In cold fury, she threatened to kill Elijah. Elijah was fearful and fled to Beersheba in the land of Judah. Going a day's journey into the wilderness, he entered into the valley of despair. Mountaintop experiences are often followed by periods of despondency — the higher the mountain, the deeper the valley. He lamented, "It is enough; now, O LORD, take away my life, for I am no better than my ancestors" (19:4).

He was ready to be done with it all, but God was not finished with Elijah. An angel of God awoke Elijah and told him to consume the food and water the angel had prepared. Twice this happened. In the strength of that nourishment, Elijah traveled for forty days and nights to Mount Horeb (also know as Mount Sinai) and spent the night there in a cave.

God asked Elijah what he was doing. Elijah answered, "I have been very zealous for the LORD, the God of hosts; for the Israelites have forsaken your covenant, thrown down your altars, and killed your prophets with the sword. I alone am left, and they are seeking my life, to take it away" (19:10).

These words had some degree of truth to them, but they were the words of a man in the dark pit of depression. When a person is deeply depressed, he or she can only see the dark side of things. Hope flees and death and despair sit close at hand. Thoughts lead to darkness rather than to light. Left alone, the darkness only deepens.

God did not leave Elijah alone. As Elijah was in the cave, the LORD came to him. There was a great wind, splitting rocks in pieces, followed by an earthquake and then a fire, but the LORD was not in any of these. Such events of power would dazzle a normal person, but for a person in the depths of depression, these are merely more signs of negativity.

Then there came a sound of sheer silence or a still, small voice. This understated sound got Elijah's attention, and he came to the mouth of the cave. God and Elijah spoke together. God listened to Elijah's lament, and then God gave Elijah an assignment to anoint new kings over Aram and Israel and to anoint Elisha to succeed Elijah as prophet. Through these new kings, God would put an end to the house of Ahab. God also gave Elijah this assurance: "Yet I will leave seven thousand in Israel, all the knees that have not bowed to Baal, and every mouth that has not kissed him" (19:18). The antidote to depression was having a meaningful purpose to serve.

According to the word of the LORD that Elijah spoke, evil Ahab was killed in battle and wicked Jezebel was thrown to her death from a tower in Jezreel. So ended the house of Ahab.

For thought or discussion:

- Have you ever had a mountaintop experience that gave you a new vision?
- Has that vision been challenged as you dealt with the everyday things of life?
- Have you experienced depression, and if so, what was it that restored your hope?

31. Passing the Mantle

Elijah to Elisha
2 Kings 2

As God had directed Elijah on Mount Horeb, Elijah returned to Israel, renewed in the power of the LORD, and anointed new kings for both Aram and Israel. He also called Elisha to leave his parents' home and to became Elijah's servant and protege.

Sometime later, when Elijah knew that the time of his departure was at hand, the two men prepared to leave Gilgal and go to Bethel. Elijah encouraged Elisha to remain in Gilgal, but Elisha said, "As the LORD lives, and as you yourself live, I will not leave you" (2:2). They went on together.

When they came to Bethel, a group of prophets came to Elisha and asked him if he knew that the LORD was going to take Elijah away from him. Elisha said that he knew it.

Elijah urged Elisha to remain in Bethel while he himself went on to Jericho. Elisha replied as he had in Gilgal. The two traveled on to Jericho. Another company of prophets asked Elisha, "'Do you know that today the LORD will take your master away from you?' And he answered, 'Yes, I know; be silent'" (2:5).

Yet again, in Jericho, Elijah encouraged Elisha to remain there as he went, at the LORD's direction, to the Jordan. Same reply from Elisha.

When the two men came to the River Jordan, Elijah rolled up his mantle and struck the water. The water was parted and the two prophets crossed on dry ground. Then Elijah asked what he could do for Elisha before being taken from him. Elisha asked to receive a double portion of Elijah's spirit. "You have asked a hard thing; yet, if you see me as I am being taken from you, it will be granted you" (2:10).

As they continued walking and talking, a chariot of fire and horses of fire separated them, and Elijah was taken up into heaven in a whirlwind. Elisha exclaimed, "Father, father! The chariots of Israel and its horsemen!" (2:12).

When Elisha could no longer see Elijah, he picked up Elijah's mantle, returned to the Jordan, struck the water so that it parted, crossed on dry ground, and came to the company of prophets at Jericho. They exclaimed, "The spirit of Elijah rests on Elisha" (2:15).

Thinking that God may have swept Elijah away to some distant valley or mountain, the prophets begged to send fifty men to search for Elijah. Though Elisha sought to dissuade them, they searched for three days but found nothing. In fact, Elijah had been taken alive into heaven (another foreshadowing of a future event), and Elisha was to carry on in Israel, speaking for God.

For thought or discussion:

- Have you had the experience of needing to pass on a project or position to someone else?
- Have you been the one who inherited a project of position from someone else?
- In either case, what were the challenges and how did you either struggle or thrive?

32. The Power of the Small

Naaman and Elisha
2 Kings 5

She was a young Israelite girl who by her words brought unexpected blessings.

We don't know her name. The only things we do know about her are that she had been carried away by the Arameans on one of their raids into Israel, and that she served the wife of a man named Naaman. Having been stolen from her home and placed in servitude, this young girl could have wished for nothing but the worst for her captors. But that is not what happened.

Naaman was the commander of the army of the king of Aram. He was a mighty warrior and held in high esteem, but he also suffered with leprosy.

One day the young slave girl said to her mistress, "If only my lord were with the prophet who is in Samaria! He would cure him of his leprosy" (5:3). So Naaman told this to the king, and the king of Aram sent him to Israel with silver and gold and garments and a letter to the king of Israel. The letter read, "When this letter reaches you, know that I have sent to you my servant Naaman, that you may cure him of his leprosy" (5:6).

Imagine King Joram's horror. How was he supposed to cure Naaman's leprosy? Clearly, he thought, the king of Aram was trying to pick a fight. What was King Joram to do?

When Elisha heard of the king's dismay, he told the king to send Naaman to him so that Naaman could learn that there was a prophet, a man of God, in Israel. The king was beyond relieved to pass this problem on to someone else.

So Naaman and his whole company came to Elisha's house with their horses and chariots. It must have been an awesome sight and sound — the stomping and blowing of the war horses and the rattle and clatter of chariots and weaponry. A powerful man had come to visit.

Naaman expected that the prophet would come out, dramatically call on God, wave his hand, and cure his leprosy. Instead, Elisha sent a messenger to instruct Naaman to go and bathe seven times in the river Jordan and be restored. Naaman left in a huff, grumbling that the rivers of Damascus were surely far superior to any river in Israel.

Naaman's servants, however, reasoned with him. If Elisha had commanded him to do something difficult, would he not have done it? Why not do this simple thing? And so Naaman did as Elisha had directed. He immersed himself seven times in the River Jordan, and his flesh was restored like that of a youth. He was clean!

In gratitude, Naaman returned to Elisha's house with his whole entourage. He said to the man of God, "Now I know that there is no God in all the earth except in Israel; please accept a present from your servant" (5:15). Elisha declined Naaman's repeated offers of reward. God's acts of mercy were not for sale nor were they for the prophet's gain.

Naaman asked if he could take some soil with him to Damascus so that he could prepare a place where he would henceforth offer sacrifices only to the Lord. He also asked for ongoing pardon for the times he would be asked to escort his king into the house of the god Rimmon for worship. Elisha said, "Go in peace" (5:19). Naaman left for home, a changed and renewed man.

Elisha had a servant named Gehazi. This man had witnessed all that had transpired, and he could not believe that the prophet let Naaman go without exacting a price. Gehazi ran after Naaman. Telling him that two visitors had come to Elisha (which was not true), he requested a talent of silver and two changes of clothing for the visitors. Naaman gladly gave him the clothing and two talents of silver. Gehazi took them and stowed them in a safe place for his own later use.

When Elisha asked Gehazi where he had gone, the servant said that he had gone nowhere. But Elisha said, "Did I not go with you in spirit when someone left his chariot to meet you? Is this a time to accept money and to accept clothing…? Therefore, the leprosy of Naaman shall cling to you, and to your descendants forever" (5:26-27).

While Gehazi's greed brought him to grief, Naaman returned to Damascus with joy and thanksgiving, and Elisha carried on faithfully as a devoted man of God.

The unnamed Israelite slave girl spoke simple words that brought this all to fruition.

For thought or discussion:

- Has anyone ever spoken a word of unexpected blessing to you?
- How important have you found the little things of life to be? What is an example?
- When did you have the opportunity to speak a word that changed someone else's life?
- Most of God's directives are fairly basic. Why are they so often ignored while we wait for God to command us to do particularly challenging things?

33. Foiling the Fire's Might

Shadrach, Meshach, and Abednego
Daniel 3

King Nebuchadnezzar of Babylon was a mighty king, conquerer, and ruler of lands near and far. He wanted to be sure that everyone knew of his might and glory. Therefore, he made a golden statue and set it up in the plain of Dura. The golden image was nine feet wide and ninety feet high. It was glorious to behold, but beholding it was not enough. What good is a statue without people to adore or worship it?

Nebuchadnezzar assembled all of the officials of his kingdom to the plain of Dura for the dedication of the golden image. Then the king's herald announced, "When you hear the sound of the horn, pipe, lyre, trigon, harp, drum, and entire musical ensemble, you are to fall down and worship the golden statue that King Nebuchadnezzar has set up. Whoever does not fall down and worship shall immediately be thrown into a furnace of blazing fire" (3:5-6).

What would you have done? The obvious choice was to bow down and worship, for the alternative was less than desirable. The music played, and the people bowed down to the golden statue. Nebuchadnezzar was pleased.

He was pleased until it was brought to his attention that three of his officials had not worshiped the statue. Those three men were Jews, among the strong and able young men taken in captivity from Judah; and their Babylonian names were Shadrach, Meshach, and Abednego. (Their Hebrew names were Hananiah, Mishael, and Azariah.)

Enraged, Nebuchadnezzar confronted the three men and asked if it was true they had refused to serve his gods and worship his image. He said that if they would worship the golden image, all would be well; but if not, it would be the fiery furnace for them, "and who is the god that will deliver you out of my hands?" (3:15).

Boldly Shadrach, Meshach, and Abednego answered, "If our God whom we serve is able to deliver us from the furnace of blazing fire and out of your hand, O king, let him deliver us. But if not, be it known to you, O King, that we will not serve your gods and we will not worship the golden statue that you have set up" (3:17-18).

The king was so enraged that he ordered the furnace to be heated to seven times its normal heat and the three men to be bound and thrown into the fire. So hot was the fire that the guards who threw Shadrach, Meshach, and Abednego into the fire were themselves killed by the flames.

Suddenly King Nebuchadnezzar jumped to his feet. Three men had been thrown into the furnace, but he saw four men walking unhurt in the midst of the fire. The fourth, he said, "has the appearance of a god" (3:25). He called for the men to come out of the furnace, and out walked Shadrach, Meshach, and Abednego. Not a hair of their heads was singed, their clothing was unharmed, and not even the smell of smoke came from them.

A powerful king had just witnessed a power far beyond his imagining. He declared, "Blessed be the God of Shadrach, Meshach, and Abednego, who has sent his angel and delivered his servants who trusted in him. They disobeyed the king's command and yielded up their bodies rather than serve and worship any god except their own God" (3:28). He then decreed that anyone who spoke against the LORD would be destroyed; and he promoted Shadrach, Meshach, and Abednego to positions of great honor.

For thought or discussion:

- What shiny object has garnered your attention and caused you to be amazed?
- What do you consider to be worthy of your adoration?
- For what would you be willing to die?

34. Safe Among the Lions

Daniel
Daniel 6

Here is another story of jealousy, intrigue, pride, faithfulness, regret, and deliverance.

Darius was the king of the Medes and the Persians. He had appointed 127 officials called satraps and stationed them throughout his kingdom. Over the satraps there were three presidents to whom the satraps reported. One of the presidents was Daniel. Like Shadrach, Meshach, and Abednego, Daniel was a stellar young man of Judah who had been taken captive by Nebuchadnezzar.

Before long, Daniel distinguished himself so that, as it had been for Joseph in Egypt, Darius planned to appoint Daniel over all the kingdom. The other two presidents and the 127 satraps were jealous and sought to bring about Daniel's demise.

Since Daniel was a man of honor and integrity, the presidents and satraps could find no corruption, malfeasance, or negligence with which to charge him. They concluded, "We shall not find any ground for complaint against this Daniel unless we find it in connection with the law of his God" (6:5). They hatched a plan.

The men approached the king and told him that they were all in agreement that Darius should issue an edict "that whoever prays to anyone, divine or human, for thirty days, except to you, O king, shall be thrown into a den of lions" (6:7). They also reminded Darius that according to the law of the Medes and the Persians, such a decree could not be revoked.

King Darius, filled with pride, put his signature on the document. It is all too often the case that the reason behind a request or the ramifications of an action are not fully examined before taking action. Flattery easily blinds the eyes.

Daniel knew full well that the king had signed the edict. Nevertheless, as was his custom, he continued to pray to the LORD three times each day. He would go into his house, face toward Jerusalem, and kneel to pray and praise God. At one such time, the conspirators found him praying.

When Darius was informed of this, he was deeply distressed. This was not because his pride was wounded, but rather because of his love and regard for Daniel. The king regretted making such a foolish edict, and he sought a way to save Daniel.

The accusers, driven by jealousy, would have none of it; and they reminded the king repeatedly that the edict could not be revoked. The end result was that Daniel was thrown into the den of lions. Darius said to Daniel, "May your God, whom you faithfully serve, deliver you!" (6:16). A stone was placed over the mouth of the den and sealed with the signets of the king and of the officials. Darius went to his palace and spent the night fasting and sleepless.

At daybreak, the king hurried to the den, hoping against hope to find that his worst fears were unfounded. He called out, "O Daniel, servant of the living God, has your God whom you faithfully serve been able to deliver you from the lions?" (6:20).

To his great relief, Daniel answered from within the den, "My God sent his angel and shut the lions' mouths so that they would not hurt me, because I was found blameless before him; and also before you, O king, I have done no wrong" (6:22).

In great joy, Darius commanded that Daniel be taken up out of the den of lions. He also commanded that Daniel's accusers be thrown into the lions' den. It did not go well for them there.

The king issued a new decree that "in all my royal dominion people should tremble and fear before the God of Daniel: For he is the living God, enduring forever…he works signs and wonders in heaven and on earth; for he has saved Daniel from the power of the lions" (6:26-27).

Daniel prospered.

For thought or discussion:

- Are you aware of a time when flattery clouded the judgment of either you or someone else?
- Have you ever regretted a decision you made?
- How do you remain faithful when other people work against you?

35. God's Foreign Chosen Instrument

Cyrus the Persian
2 Chronicles 36 / Ezra 1

Whenever the Israelites embarked on paths of disobedience, God brought upon them the consequence of their actions. We saw that, among other places, in the Book of Judges and in the division and demise of the northern and southern kingdoms. The northern kingdom was destroyed by the Assyrians, and the southern kingdom was taken into captivity by the Babylonians. God used foreign rulers, not because of their might or righteousness, but because of his purposes and by his permission, to mete out judgment on his chosen people.

The Assyrian Empire was conquered by the Babylonians, and the Babylonians were conquered by the Medes and Persians (who in turn were conquered by the Greeks — but that's another story). The ruler of the Persians was a man named Cyrus, and he became God's instrument to bring about the restoration of Judah.

In the first year of Cyrus' reign, the LORD stirred up the spirit of the king to issue an edict. Cyrus sent a herald throughout his kingdom to proclaim: "The LORD, the God of heaven, has given me all the kingdoms of the earth, and he has charged me to build him a house at Jerusalem in Judah. Any of those among you who are of his people…are now permitted to go up to Jerusalem in Judah, and rebuild the house of the LORD, the God of Israel." (Ezra 1:2-3) He also directed that those who chose to go should be aided by their neighbors with silver, gold, goods, animals, and freewill offerings for the house of God in Jerusalem. (Here is an echo of the departure of the Israelites from Egypt centuries earlier.)

Cyrus himself brought out all the vessels of the house of the LORD that Nebuchadnezzar had carried away from Jerusalem. He put these in the care of a trustworthy man, Sheshbazzar, who brought them back to Jerusalem to be placed in the temple when it had been rebuilt.

Since the time between the deportation to Babylon and Cyrus' edict of restoration had been seventy years, most of those who were encouraged to move to Judah had never seen that land. They had no personal memory of the temple, or of the city of Jerusalem, or of the towns and villages, or of the country itself. They only knew what they had been told by their elders about the wonders of the past.

A total of 42,360 descendants of Judah and Benjamin (plus their servants and animals) emigrated to the land of Judah and resettled the land. They were faced with the monumental task of rebuilding the house of God in Jerusalem, of erecting again the walls of the city, of restoring all the towns that had been left in ruins, and of renewing fields, orchards, and vineyards. But thanks to God's foreign chosen instrument, King Cyrus of Persia, they were home again.

For thought or discussion:

- How do you think you would have responded to Cyrus' edict if the place you were living was the only home you had ever known?
- Do you imagine that arriving in the land of Judah was more fulfillment or disappointment?
- Do you have stories of your own ancestors moving to new lands and opportunities?

36. Reluctant Rescuer

Esther and Mordecai
Esther

Not all of the Jews, who were encouraged by King Cyrus to return to Judah, chose to go. Many remained in Persia, and it is in regard to these that this story is told.

King Ahasuerus (another name for King Xerxes) reigned over the 127 Persian provinces from India to Ethiopia. In the third year of his reign, he regaled his officials and ministers, showing off his great wealth and splendor for six months. Then, for seven days, he gave a lavish banquet for all the inhabitants in the city of Susa. Drinking was without restraint.

On the seventh day, when the king and all with him were well in their cups, Ahasuerus commanded his wife, Queen Vashti, to come to the banquet wearing her royal crown, so that all might be impressed by her great beauty. It is not clear whether Vashti was to wear her crown in addition to her gown, or more likely, to come wearing only her crown. In either case, she had no desire to be paraded in front of a room full of drunken men. She refused to come.

The king was enraged. He consulted with his sages to determine what to do. He was strongly advised to put Vashti away and to give her position to a new queen. After all, it was reasoned that if word got out that the queen had disobeyed her husband, all the noble women of the kingdom would be emboldened to treat their husbands with similar contempt. Since this was unthinkable, action needed to be taken — an edict needed to be made declaring that "every man should be master in his own house"(1:22). Drunken King Ahasuerus commanded it to be done.

With this potential rebellion of women thwarted, there remained the matter of finding a new queen. It was suggested that beautiful young virgins should be sought throughout the provinces and brought to the king's harem in Susa. There the women would be given cosmetic treatments, six months with oil of myrrh and six months with perfumes and cosmetics. "And let the girl who pleases the king be queen instead of Vashti" (2:4). King Ahasuerus agreed.

In turn, each of the virgins was brought to the king, entering his presence in the evening, remaining until morning, and then returning to a second harem. (She would remain there unless the king delighted in her and summoned her again.) We can assume that the time spent with Ahasuerus was not simply a time of conversation, inquiring about the virgin's family and friends, hobbies and wishes. The king undoubtedly had sex with the virgins so that he could see who pleased and satisfied him the most. The bad news for those not selected was that they would live out their lives in the harem. So much for dreams of love and children and freedom.

Among the women gathered for Ahasuerus was a woman named Esther. She was Jewish, but that fact was not known to the king. What was known was Esther's great beauty. She was chosen to be the new queen.

Esther's cousin, Mordecai, had watched over her since the death of her parents. Mordecai came by regularly to check on Esther. On one occasion, he overheard a plot by two of the king's eunuchs to assassinate Ahasuerus. Mordecai told this to Queen Esther and she told the king in Mordecai's name. When an investigation confirmed the plot, the conspirators were hanged, and this was all recorded in the annals of the kingdom.

A man named Haman gained the king's favor and was promoted to the highest office in the land. All the servants and officials of the king bowed down and did obeisance to Haman, as the king directed. Mordecai, being Jewish, did not bow to Haman, and this galled Haman greatly. In fact, it so angered Haman that he decided to destroy Mordecai, and for good measure, all of Mordecai's people, the Jews.

To that end, Haman cast Pur (lots) to determine on which day this destruction of the Jews in Persia would take place. The lot fell on the thirteenth day of the twelfth month. Haman then denounced the Jews to Ahasuerus and got the king to sign off on this plot.

When Mordecai learned of it, he appealed to Esther to go the the king and intercede. She was reluctant because not even she could approach the king unbidden. Mordecai said to her, "For if you keep silence at such a time as this, relief and deliverance will rise for the Jews from another quarter, but…Perhaps you have come to royal dignity for just such a time as this" (4:14).

After three days of fasting by Esther and the Jews of Susa, Esther went to the king and was thankfully welcomed. Being asked her request, she invited Ahasuerus and Haman to come to a banquet that evening. At the banquet, she asked the two of them to come to a second banquet the next evening, at which time she would make known her request to the king.

Haman was overjoyed to be so favored by Queen Esther. But once again, Mordecai's lack of respect stuck in his craw. He constructed a huge gallows on which he planned to hang Mordecai. He intended the next morning to seek the king's approval for Mordecai's execution.

Unfortunately for Haman, the king had difficulty sleeping and asked to have the annals read to him. When the account of the assassination plot was read, Ahasuerus asked if Mordecai had ever been properly rewarded. He learned that this had not been done.

When Haman approached the king the next morning, the king asked what should be done for a man the king wanted to honor. Haman, assuming that this meant him, suggested dressing the man in royal robes, putting him on the king's horse, and parading him through the streets while proclaiming "Thus shall it be done for the man whom the king wishes to honor" (6:9). This pleased the king, who directed Haman to do this for Mordecai. Imagine Haman's humiliation and how he must have gnashed his teeth as he led his enemy through the streets of the capital.

That evening, at the banquet Esther prepared for the king and Haman, Ahasuerus asked the queen for her request. She said, "Let my life be given me…and the lives of my people… for we have been sold, I and my people, to be destroyed, to be killed, and to be annihilated" (7:3-4). The king asked who was responsible for this horrible plan; and Esther said, "A foe and enemy, this wicked Haman!" (7:6).

At the king's direction, Haman was hanged on the very gallows he had erected for the hanging of Mordecai. An edict was issued instructing the Jews throughout the kingdom to arm themselves and defend themselves against all who would do them harm on the thirteenth day of the twelfth month.

Ultimately, the Jews defended themselves on that day and on the day following, and they became an honored people within Ahasuerus' kingdom. Those two days were declared a festival, the Feast of Purim, and were henceforth to be celebrated annually among the Jews, in thanksgiving for the deliverance that had come through the actions of Queen Esther.

For thought or discussion:

- Have you ever been asked to do something that totally terrified you?
- Have you ever received an honor that ultimately proved not to be a blessing to you?
- Have you ever had to take an action that required great risk?

37. God's Ways Will Prevail

Jonah
Jonah

The word of the LORD came to the prophet Jonah: "Go at once to Nineveh, that great city, and cry out against it; for their wickedness has come up before me" (1:2).

Nineveh was a major city in Mesopotamia. Since it was a foreign city, Jonah likely thought it deserved any punishment God might visit upon it. The last thing Jonah wanted to do was to seek deliverance for Nineveh. Warning one's own people was one thing; warning people of an idolatrous nation was quite another. Jonah wanted to get away in a hurry.

He went to the Mediterranean and boarded a ship in Joppa that was bound for Tarshish. Instead of going east, Jonah sailed west. It seemed good to him to put as much space between himself and Nineveh as possible. He paid his fare and ran from God.

God was not to be ignored. The LORD sent a great storm, and the ship threatened to break apart. The sailors threw the cargo into the sea to lighten the load, and each man cried out to his god for deliverance. Still the storm raged and intensified.

Meanwhile, Jonah had gone below decks and was asleep. The captain awakened him and said, "Get up, call on your god! Perhaps the god will spare us a thought so that we do not perish." (1:6) So much for thinking Jonah could outrun God.

On deck, the sailors cast lots to determine on whose account disaster stared them in the face. The lot fell on Jonah, and since he had told them previously that he was fleeing from the presence of the LORD, the sailors wondered what they should do to him to quiet the storm. He said that they should throw him overboard. They tried instead to row for land; but when they could make no headway, they asked for Jonah's forgiveness and threw him into the sea. The storm stopped.

God had a purpose for Jonah, and so he appointed a large fish to swallow him. Jonah was in the belly of the fish for three days. He thought, and prayed, and vowed to offer sacrifices of thanksgiving to the LORD in his holy temple, if his life was spared. The fish spewed Jonah out on the dry land.

Free! Except that God was not easily put off, and the word of the LORD came to Jonah a second time: "Get up, go to Nineveh, that great city, and proclaim to it the message that I tell you" (3:2).

Jonah went into Nineveh and proclaimed, "Forty days more, and Nineveh shall be overthrown!" (3:4).

Wonder of wonders, the people of Nineveh believed God's word and the warning that Jonah brought. All the people, from the king on down, put on sackcloth, repented, and fasted. Even the animals were clothed in sackcloth. The people heeded the word that Jonah spoke, and God turned his wrath away from Nineveh.

Jonah, however, was not pleased. In fact, he was downright angry. "O LORD! Is not this what I said while I was still in my own country? ...I knew that you are a gracious God and merciful, slow to anger, and abounding in steadfast love, and ready to relent from punishing" (4:2). (In other words, why did you waste my time and energy, and how could you possibly have such mercy on a city like Nineveh?)

Perhaps believing that God would come to his senses, Jonah went out east of the city and made a booth for himself where he could sit in the shade and wait to see what would become of Nineveh.

The LORD, as a lesson, made a castor bean plant grow overnight to provide welcome shade for Jonah. Jonah liked the bush. The next day, God made a worm attack the bush so that it withered. Then came a sultry east wind and intense sunshine so that Jonah was faint. He said, "It is better for me to die than to live" (4:8).

It was time for God to bring the lesson to its conclusion. God asked Jonah if it was right to be angry about the bush. Jonah replied, "Yes, angry enough to die" (4:9). Then God said, "You are concerned about the bush, for which you did not labor and which you did not grow; it came into being in a night and perished in a night. And should I not be concerned about Nineveh, that great city, in which there are more than a hundred and twenty thousand persons who do not know their right hand from their left, and also many animals?" (4:10-11).

God's mercy is at once surprising and confounding. God stands ready to forgive even when we struggle to do so, or when we cannot fathom the depth of such love and grace.

For thought or discussion:

- Has there been a time when you resisted doing what God clearly wanted you to do?
- Have you ever wished ill on another person or race or country?
- Who do you think is unworthy of God's love, grace, mercy, and forgiveness?

38. Who Was in Control?

Between the Testaments, Part 1

There are countless other stories in the Hebrew Scriptures (the thirty-nine books that Judaism divides into the Torah, the prophets, and the writings). As part of the Bible, the Hebrew scriptures are known as the Old Testament. This is not a negative term, but it differentiates the covenant God made with Israel and the covenant that was made in Jesus. Reading the New Testament without knowing the old is to miss the richness of what it means to claim that Jesus is our LORD and Savior. You are encouraged to continue to delve deeply into all the stories of the Old Testament.

The books of the Old Testament take us up to about 400 B.C., so there is a four-century gap between the two testaments. What happened in that period of time, and how does it inform the stories to which we will next turn?

Politically, there was much that changed and one thing that remained constant.

When we ended our Old Testament stories, the Persians were the masters of the world. You remember that they had conquered the Babylonians who had previously conquered the Assyrians who had conquered much of what had been the kingdom of David and Solomon. The Persians were, in turn, conquered by the forces of Alexander the Great.

Alexander was not merely a military conquerer, he was also an apostle for Hellenism, wanting to make the whole world reflect Greece. Greek became the language of commerce, Greek ways became the fashion of the day, and Greek thought sought to dominate.

When Alexander died an untimely death in 323 BC, his kingdom was divided between four of his generals: Lysimachus took control of much of Asia Minor, Cassander controlled Macedonia and Greece, Antigonus ruled much of Asia, and Ptolemy ruled Egypt and southern Syria. Israel/Palestine ultimately fell under the control of Seleucus, another one of Alexander's generals.

This division of power lasted until all the former parts of Alexander's kingdom were conquered by the Romans.

The thing that remained constant through all those changes was that the Jews were always under the control of a foreign power.

Some overlords were more tolerant than others, but the greatest conflict came when Antiochus IV Epiphanes, a descendant of Seleucus, came to power. Wanting a unified Hellenistic realm, he commanded his subjects to worship the Greek gods and to refrain from all Jewish practices. To this end, an image of Zeus was placed in the Jerusalem temple, pagan rites were celebrated, and swine were slaughtered on the altar. This became known as the Abomination of Desolation.

A Jewish revolt took place. When an altar was set up in the village of Modin, all the inhabitants were directed to make sacrifices on it to show loyalty to Antiochus. Mattathias, the elderly Jewish priest of the village, was asked to set a good example for the other villagers. He refused, and when another man came forward to offer a sacrifice, Mattathias slew both that man and the emissaries of Antiochus. Mattathias fled with his five sons and was joined by others who shared his devotion to Judaism. Ultimately, led by his son, Judas Maccabee (the Hammer), a brief period of freedom was won. During this time, having regained Jerusalem, the Maccabees cleansed the temple, removing all pagan elements. An eight-day Feast of Dedication took place, and the small flask of oil miraculously sufficed to fuel the great Menorah for all those days. This has been celebrated ever since as Hanukkah, the Festival of Lights and the Triumph of Freedom.

When we turn to the New Testament, Israel was firmly under the control of Rome.

For thought or discussion:

- How important are historical events in shaping our lives?
- What is an historical event that you have experienced that has powerfully shaped you?
- How confused are you about all of this?

39. Pharisees, Sadducees, Essenes, and Zealots

Between the Testaments, Part 2

There is a collection of writing called The Apocrypha. The name refers to the idea that these were hidden texts, only given to those initiated into a particular group. These writings, including additions to Old Testament works and stand-alone books, were written over a period of about three hundred years, primarily during the time between the testaments. While the Apocrypha is known in all Christian circles, it is not generally considered to be canonical or authoritative. It does, however, give us some corroborative information about historical events in this period, and it introduces to us some groups within Judaism that are unknown in the Old Testament.

During the time between the Testaments, there were both political and theological divisions. In response to the Hellenistic push of conquerers, a number of sects within Judaism were formed.

Many, perhaps most, of the Jews were open to the synthesis of Hellenism and Judaism, finding benefits in adding Greek dress, thought, and/or practices to their traditional ways of being. To a large extent, the Sadducees were part of this group. They were predominantly members of the Jerusalem aristocracy and of the high priesthood. By making peace with the political rulers, they attained wealth and influence. Theologically, the Sadducees honored the Torah, but they did not accept oral law and tradition. They rejected belief in resurrection and angels.

Those who most strongly resisted Hellenization were called the Hasidim, the pious ones. From this group come two sects, the Pharisees and the Essenes.

The Pharisees sought, in faithfulness to the Hebrew Scriptures, to separate themselves not from other Jews, but from the influences of Hellenism. Seeking to understand the teachings of antiquity in relation to the challenges of their own time, they turned to the scriptural interpretations of learned rabbis. Valuing the oral traditions of the various rabbis, and seeking to be faithful in life and practice, Pharisees did not always agree on specifics. What they did agree on was the desire to live as faithful and observant Jews. As the Sadducees were dominant in the temple and its affairs, the Pharisees' domain was the synagogue.

The Essenes were far more radical than the Pharisees. They sought to separate themselves not only from Hellenism but also from other non-orthodox Jews. Essenes, for the most part lived in monastic communities and followed strict rules of conduct and of piety. Most of these communities required celibacy, but others apparently allowed married members. Essenes rejected the Jerusalem priesthood and regarded their own communities as the true Israel.

A famous example of the Essenes was the Qumran community. The discovery of the Dead Sea scrolls in the Judean wilderness near En Gedi in the 1940s shed great light on this community and on this complex period of history.

The books of the Apocrypha and many other non-biblical writings were influential in the Essene communities. These believers tended to have a strong apocalyptic emphasis, looking toward the final consummation of all things. In most cases, there was the conviction that final deliverance would come to the members of the community while the rest of the defiled Jews and all other people would be swept away.

There were also Jews identified as Zealots. While Roman rule was not welcomed by most Jews, the majority of people saw it either as God's punishment for unfaithfulness or simply as the way things were in the world. Zealots, on the other hand, were so radically committed to the LORD God and opposed to Rome, that they resisted anything that would demonstrate loyalty to Caesar. Such Jews were willing to use violence against their overlords, acting as God's agents of righteous wrath against idolatry. It is likely that the actions of the Zealots were instrumental in causing Rome to bring its heel down hard upon Israel.

Pharisees, Sadducees, Essenes, and Zealots do not appear in the texts of the Old Testament. Pharisees and Sadducees are mentioned frequently in the New Testament. Zealots are infrequently (and Essenes never) mentioned in the text of the New

Testament. All four groups, however, appear in many non-canonical writings of the period, and they were all active and influential at the turn of the era.

While each group may have had prior antecedents, they came into definitive existence in the time between the Testaments.

For thought or discussion:

- If you had lived in the time between the testaments, do you think that you would have identified with any of these groups?
- Do you see similarities between any of these sects and any religious groups today?

40. Fascinated by the Begats

Matthew 1:1-17

When a person is encouraged to read the Bible and decides to do so, the logical place to start is at the beginning. As you have seen through the stories recounted so far, while the reader may have ample reasons for confusion, the Book of Genesis is full of stories and there is an ongoing narrative. This continues through the first half of the Book of Exodus, and then the narrative seems to be replaced by laws and by instructions for building and furnishing the tabernacle and for providing outfits for the priests. Often as not, that is where a person's reading grinds to a halt.

The next idea might be to bypass the Old Testament and launch into reading the New Testament. Once again, it seems logical to start at the beginning. What the reader finds is a genealogy filled with unknown and hard to pronounce names. What's a person to do?

You may or may not be interested in genealogy; but if you take time to read through this list of names, you will recognize some of them from the stories you have already read in the Old Testament. Right off the bat, you will see that Jesus (who is the subject of almost all the remaining stories) is identified as the Messiah or Christ and that he was descended from David and Abraham — David, the greatest king, and Abraham, the father of promise.

Verses 7-11 list the kings of Judah. Verses 12-16 continue the line of David after Cyrus the Persian allowed the Jews to return from captivity in Babylon. Each person had a life and a story, but for our purposes, there are three things that are especially important about this genealogy: the continuation of the chosen people, the women included, and God's wonderful faithfulness in spite of human failure.

In the King James Version of the Bible, this passage is translated, "Abraham begat Isaac; and Isaac begat Jacob..." While the NRSV translation, "Abraham was the father of Isaac, and Isaac the father of Jacob..." (1:2). seems clearer, there is something compelling about that old word "begat." What one begets is of the same substance as oneself. A cat begets a kitten, not a gosling. A cow begets a calf, not a puppy. There is the declaration here that from Abraham onward, each generation begat a new generation that was of the same nature and substance as itself. Sinful humans begat sinful humans, and the sinful chosen people begat more sinful chosen people.

Typical of genealogies of its time, this is a list of fathers and sons. Interestingly, however, there are four women named in the list (in addition to Mary at its conclusion). Why are Tamar, Rahab, Ruth, and the wife of Uriah mentioned? What are we to learn from them?

You have read the story of Rahab the prostitute of Jericho. She hid the spies sent by Joshua, and in turn, she and her family were saved when Jericho was destroyed. She became the mother of Boaz.

Ruth, the Moabite, was loyal to her mother-in-law, Naomi; and she married Boaz and became the mother of Obed, the grandfather of King David. Neither Rahab nor Ruth were Israelites, but they became part of God's chosen people and integral links in the genealogy of Jesus.

You remember the story of King David's seduction of Bathsheba, the wife of Uriah, and David's arranged murder of her husband. In spite of this, their second son, Solomon, was the one through whom the promise was continued.

And then there is the equally seedy story of Tamar and Judah (Genesis chapter 38), a story of deception and incest. Tamar was the widow of Judah's oldest son, Er. When Er died, Judah gave his second son, Onan, to Tamar. He also died, and Judah promised to give his third son, Shelah, to Tamar. But he did not do so. Tamar disguised herself as a prostitute and had sex with Judah. She became pregnant. Judah was incensed; but when she gave proof that he was the father, he declared that he had been more in the wrong than she, for he had not kept his promise to her. The result of the pregnancy was the birth of twins, Perez and Zerah. The promise of God went through Perez.

The greatest lesson to learn from this genealogy is that God's plans and promises are not derailed by sinful people. There is not a person in this genealogy who is perfect. All these people, though some were far more esteemed and faithful than others, were ordinary people with failures aplenty and feet of clay. As we have looked at the stories of many of these people, that fact should be abundantly clear. God did not condone adultery, murder, deceit, incest, idolatry, or any of the other sins these people committed. Nevertheless, God used each of them, not because of their deserving, but because of his mercy and purposes.

If God has kept his promises generation after generation, in spite of all of the messiness of the lives of all of these people, why should we doubt that God will keep his promises to us as well?

For thought or discussion:

- With whom in this genealogy do you most identify?
- Have you paid attention to your own genealogy?
- Are there people in your lineage or family who make you proud or cause you embarrassment?

41. Of Angels, Old Age, and Unbelief

Zechariah and Elizabeth
Luke 1

Zechariah and Elizabeth were a godly couple. They were descended from priests, and Zechariah was a priest. Both were getting on in years, and in spite of their prayers, they had no children. But that was to change.

One day, when Zechariah was serving in the temple, it was his turn to enter the sanctuary and offer the incense. As he did so, an angel of the Lord appeared to him. You might think that it would be good to have an angel appear to you, but Zechariah was terrified!

Angels are God's messengers or agents. It is common in art to depict them with wings or as cute cherubs. In Christmas programs, angels are usually girls in white robes with wings and glittery haloes. This gives the impression that angels are sweet and altogether benign.

The Bible gives quite another picture of these divine beings. Angels sometimes appear in winged form, but they may also appear in more normal human form. However, they appear, there is something awesome about angels. Throughout the Bible, the normal reaction of people when confronted by an angel is fear or even terror. Angels exude power and strength and holiness.

Angels appear in several of the next stories.

The angel told Zechariah not to be afraid. He announced that the prayers of Zechariah and Elizabeth had been heard, and that they would have a son who was to be named John. He also instructed Zechariah that the boy was never to drink wine or strong drink, that he would be filled with the Holy Spirit, and that he would "make ready a people prepared for the Lord" (1:17). Like Sampson and Samuel (whose stories have already been told), John was to be a Nazarite from birth.

Like Sarah, long ago, who laughed at the idea that she, in her old age, would bear a child, Zechariah responded, "How will I know that this is so? For I am an old man, and my wife is getting on in years." (1:18) It sounds like a reasonable enough question, but behind the words was disbelief. The angel replied, "I am Gabriel. I stand in the presence of God, and I have been sent to speak to you and to bring you this good news. But now, because you did not believe my words, which will be fulfilled in their time, you will become mute, unable to speak, until the day these things occur" (1:19-20).

When Zechariah came out of the temple, it was clear to the people that he had seen a vision. He finished his shift and then went home. On his way, he likely wondered how he was to explain all of this to Elizabeth, especially since he could not speak. How was he going to explain the angel and the promises? How was he going to own up to his unwillingness to believe?

However, he communicated the event to Elizabeth, the angel's words came true. Elizabeth conceived, and (again like Sarah before her) she marveled at the goodness and grace of God that enabled her to bear a child. When the baby was born, her friends and relatives rejoiced with her.

On the eighth day, when the boy was to be circumcised, the people thought that he should be named Zechariah after his father. Elizabeth said that his name was to be John. The people protested that none of their relatives had that name, so they turned to Zechariah to have him weigh in on the matter. He asked for a writing tablet, and on it he wrote, "His name is John." (1:63)

Immediately, Zechariah's tongue was freed and he began to speak, praising God. The people were absolutely amazed, and the question began to circulate throughout the area, "What then will this child become?" (1:66).

Zechariah, filled with the Holy Spirit, uttered a prophecy which partly answered the question. "And you, child, will be called the prophet of the most high; for you will go before the Lord to prepare his ways, to give knowledge of salvation to his people by the forgiveness of their sins" (1:76-77).

The fulfillment of these words is another story soon to be told.

For thought or discussion:

- Do you believe that angels exist in our world today? Why or why not?
- Do you think that we are ever too old or too young for God to use us for his good purposes?
- For what surprising thing in your life do you find yourself praising God?

42. Chosen Handmaid of the Lord

Mary
Luke 1:26-56

Mary was Jewish, devout, young, engaged to be married, a kinswoman of Elizabeth, a resident of Nazareth, and uniquely chosen by God.

In the sixth month of Elizabeth's pregnancy, the same angel Gabriel who had appeared to Zechariah, came to Mary. Gabriel said, "Greetings, favored one! The Lord is with you" (1:28). Whatever did that mean? Surely, she lived in the confidence that the God of Israel was with her just as God was with all of her people, but what did "favored one" mean? It is altogether likely that she thought of herself as an ordinary person and that her aspirations were to marry, raise a family, and be as faithful to God as she possibly could be. It is interesting that the appearance of Gabriel was more perplexing than terrifying to her.

Gabriel continued with the message he was sent to bring, and what a momentous message it was. "And now, you will conceive in your womb and bear a son, and you will name him Jesus. He will be great and will be called the Son of the most high, and the Lord God will give to him the throne of his ancestor David. He will reign over the house of Jacob forever, and of his kingdom there will be no end" (1:31-33).

Mary responded with the question, "How can this be, since I am a virgin?" (1:34). Unlike Zechariah, whose question expressed disbelief, Mary's question was about how this was to occur. As is so often the case, the attitude of the heart is more important than the specific words spoken.

Gabriel said, "The Holy Spirit will come upon you, and the power of the most high will overshadow you; therefore, the child to be born will be holy; he will be called Son of God" (1:35).

As a sign to Mary, the angel told her that once-barren Elizabeth was in her sixth month.

Mary's response was the epitome of faith and of her willingness to do the Lord's bidding. She said, "Behold, I am the handmaid of the Lord; let it be to me according to your word" (1:38

RSV). Without knowing what all this would mean and what the future would hold, she said, "Yes" to God.

Soon after this, Mary traveled alone from Nazareth in Galilee to the hill country of Judea (a distance of over eighty miles requiring at least four days) to visit her kinswoman, Elizabeth, and when she entered Elizabeth's house, the child in Elizabeth's womb jumped for joy. Elizabeth exclaimed, "Blessed are you among women, and blessed is the fruit of your womb. And why has this happened to me, that the mother of my Lord comes to me? ...And blessed is she who believed that there would be a fulfillment of what was spoken to her by the Lord" (1:42-43, 45). Here was powerful affirmation of Gabriel's words.

Mary responded with wonderful words of praise to God (known as The Magnificat) that began, "My soul magnifies the Lord, and my spirit rejoices in God my Savior, for he has looked with favor on the lowliness of his servant. Surely, from now on all generations will call me blessed; for the Mighty One has done great things for me, and holy is his name" (1:46-49).

Mary stayed with Elizabeth for three months. What do you suppose those two women, one old and one young, talked about? What wisdom did Elizabeth impart to Mary? What help was Mary to Elizabeth? Did they talk about Gabriel's visitations, the promises given, and the wonder of being given special callings? No doubt they talked about pregnancy, labor, delivery, and the joy that each expected in the birth of a son.

Mary went home just before Elizabeth's baby was due. She went home knowing that it would soon be seen that she was pregnant. She knew that there would be questions and perhaps clucking tongues in Nazareth. She went remembering the words of Gabriel and the words and counsel of Elizabeth. Above all, she went knowing that she was the one chosen by God to bear the Messiah.

Mary was not a holy woman, and therefore chosen. Rather, because God chose her, she is rightly called holy — set apart.

For thought or discussion:

- Would you have responded to Gabriel's announcement as readily as Mary did?
- What anticipations do you think Mary had as she thought about her promised son?
- Have you been blessed by the counsel and encouragement of an older mentor?

(In church tradition, on liturgical calendars, and in religious art, Gabriel's coming to Mary is known as The Annunciation [celebrated on March 25]; Mary's visit with Elizabeth is known as The Visitation [celebrated on May 31].)

43. Guardian, Steadfast and True

Joseph
Matthew 1

What is a man to do when he learns that the woman to whom he is engaged is pregnant, and he knows that he is not the father? That was the dilemma facing Joseph. He was a good and honorable man, and learning such news must have troubled him sorely. What would you have done if you were Joseph? Would anger or betrayal or humiliation have been your dominant feeling?

In that time, according to the law, Joseph could have brought an accusation against Mary, and if the charge was confirmed, she could have been put to death. That is not what Joseph wanted. He was determined to put her aside, but to do so quietly so that she would not be disgraced. That was likely not an easy decision for Joseph. How he planned to both dismiss her and not disgrace her was unclear, but it was what he had decided to do.

Once again, an angel from God changed the course of action. This time the angel of the Lord came in a dream. This unnamed angel said, "Joseph, son of David, do not be afraid to take Mary as your wife, for the child conceived in her is from the Holy Spirit. She shall bear a son, and you are to name him Jesus, for he will save his people from their sins" (1:20-21).

Might this have seemed like quite a stretch to Joseph? After all, who ever heard of a woman getting pregnant without the involvement of a man? Was such a thing to be even imagined, let alone believed?

When Joseph awoke, he believed that what had been revealed to him was true. He took Mary to be his wife. Beyond that, believing that the child she carried was unique in all the world, he refrained from having marital relations with Mary until after the child had been born.

In the meantime, since Joseph had not put Mary away, the people of Nazareth undoubtedly assumed that he and Mary had simply been a bit hasty. They would not have been the first couple to have a hard time waiting for their wedding night to have intercourse. But Joseph knew the truth, and he believed the word of the Lord. He knew that his ongoing assignment was going to be to support his wife and this special son, not his own, who was the fulfilling of God's promise.

He could have walked away, refusing to believe. The fact that he did not walk away means that he believed that Mary's pregnancy was from God. Through the years, many have questioned the reality of the virgin birth, but the man closest to the event — the man who had the most reason to doubt this assertion — believed that it was God's own truth. He believed that this baby was begotten of God. (Remember our earlier discussion of begat?)

There is more to Joseph's steadfast and true story, and we will soon come to that.

For thought or discussion:

- Have you ever been asked to accept something that was hard to believe?
- Has a dream ever been so real to you that it changed your mind or your actions?
- Has there been a person who quietly and steadfastly stood by you in challenging times?

44. Night of Wonder

The Birth of Jesus
Luke 2:1-20

Once upon a darksome night, while angels waited rank on rank, and all creation held its breath, God kissed the world with love.

The time leading up to that night of wonder had been less than wonderful. The Emperor Augustus had decreed a registration of his empire for the purpose of taxation. To accomplish this, each man was required to go to his ancestral home and to be enrolled along with his family. This meant that Joseph and Mary had to travel ninety miles from Nazareth in Galilee to the town of Bethlehem in Judea. This would have been an arduous journey at any time, but it must have been especially difficult for Mary, whether she walked or rode a donkey, since she was very late in her pregnancy.

To make matters worse, since the descendants of David were numerous, the town of Bethlehem was already filled with travelers when Joseph and Mary arrived. Inn after inn had no vacancy. They were fortunate to find a space in a stable. There was a bit of good news in this, for the stable would have provided a degree of privacy and quiet; it is likely that clean straw would have been available for bedding.

It was there that Mary gave birth to her son, Jesus. The Son of the most high was born in a most lowly setting. He who was to inherit the throne of David, was born far from any palace. He who would later identify himself as the Bread of Life, was born in a town called House of Bread. All of this was just as God intended it to be.

The wonder of this birth was understated to be sure, but wonder broke forth in nearby fields. Never before or since has there been a birth announcement to rival this one. Surprisingly, it was not delivered to the high and mighty of the world but to the lowest of the low.

Shepherds were among the lowest workers, and they were often distrusted and viewed with suspicion. On that night, the shepherds tending the flocks in the Bethlehem fields, experienced terror, wonder, and joy.

Again, it began with an angel. The angel of the Lord stood before the shepherds, God's glory surrounded them, and they were terrified. The angel said, "Do not be afraid; for see — I am bringing you good news of great joy for all the people: to you is born this day in the city of David a Savior, who is the Messiah, the Lord. This will be a sign for you: you will find a child wrapped in bands of cloth and lying in a manger" (2:10-12). And as if that was not awesome enough, suddenly the angel was joined by "a multitude of the heavenly host, praising God and saying, 'Glory to God in the highest heaven, and on earth peace among those whom he favors'" (2:13-14). Lest we miss the impact of that moment, the angel host was not a gathering of girls in white robes; it was the very army of heaven. Here was power beyond description. Here was a birth announcement filled with glory, light, might, and majesty.

When the shepherds recovered, they went to Bethlehem to check it out for themselves. They found Jesus, wrapped in cloths and lying in a manger. He was attended by his royal entourage: Mary, Joseph, and the animals of the stable.

The shepherds left that stable glorifying God and telling everyone they met what they had seen and heard. Most who heard them likely missed the wonder of their news because they wondered instead what the shepherds had been drinking or how they could have come up with such a fanciful tale.

But the shepherds knew what they had experienced in the fields and what they had seen in the stable. Their lives were changed. This life-changing message would eventually be spread to every corner of the world and to people of every race and station just as the angel had declared, "I am bringing you good news of great joy for all the people."

Once upon a darksome night, when evil reigned, and peace had fled, and people's lives were filled with dread, God bared his arm to save.

Once upon a darksome night, God's saving might was veiled in flesh; and humble, helpless, laid on straw, God showed the world his face.

So break into our darksome night with your pure gift of love and light, and turn our hearts to cherish most the gift of your dear Son.

For thought or discussion:

- Is there a Christmas carol that especially touches your heart with wonder and joy?
- Why do you think God entered the world in such a humble fashion?
- Have you received a Christmas gift that powerfully moved and blessed you?

(In church tradition and on liturgical calendars, the Nativity of our Lord [Christmas] is celebrated on December 25, and Christmas Eve is December 24. The Christmas Season is twelve days in length, ending on January 5. The liturgical color is white.)

45. Follow That Star

The Visit of the Magi and its Aftermath
Matthew 2

They came from the east, following a star, to kneel in adoration before the newborn king.

The Magi (astrologers or wisemen) traveled from their homeland (perhaps in Persia) to Judea because the heavens had revealed to them that a new Jewish king had been born. The logical place to go to adore a royal child was to the palace in Jerusalem. So there they went.

When King Herod heard the news, he was frightened and not at all pleased. He knew he had no new son, and the last thing he wanted was an outsider seeking to claim his throne. Who was this pretender? Where was he?

He turned to the Jewish religious leaders for answers to his questions. They found the answer to the location in the scroll of the Old Testament prophet Micah. "And you, Bethlehem, in the land of Judah, are by no means least among the rulers of Judah; for from you shall come a ruler who is to shepherd my people Israel" (2:6).

Herod met secretly with the Magi to point them to Bethlehem and to learn the exact time that the star had appeared. He sent them on their way with instructions to return to him when they had found the child. He said that he too wanted to go and pay his respects.

Leaving Jerusalem, the Magi traveled south to Bethlehem, following the star until it stopped over the house where Jesus was. In great joy, they entered, knelt in homage, and presented precious gifts of gold, frankincense, and myrrh. Then warned in a dream not to return to Jerusalem, the magi went home by another route.

Before we turn to the aftermath of this visit, let us unpack the story a bit more.

What was the nature of the star that led the wisemen to Jesus? Since the Magi were astrologers, it has been surmised that the movement of the planets within the constellations had led them to conclude that something of great importance had occurred in Judea. What would be more momentous than the birth of a king? This, however, does not account for the reappearance of the star and its stopping over the house in Bethlehem. On the other hand, the portrayal of the star in many paintings of the nativity or of the adoration of the magi, seems unlikely. If the star had been like a singular beacon in the sky, would not everyone, in great curiosity, have been drawn to the house? While we cannot know for sure what the Magi saw, it is clear that they were led by God to Bethlehem, and they were the first representatives of the nations to adore the Christ-child.

How many wisemen were there? Because there were three gifts mentioned, the assumption has been that there were three. They have even been given a variety of names from as early as the sixth century. The most commonly used were popularized by Gian Carlo Menotti in "Amahl and the Night Visitors," where they are called kings: Kaspar, Melchior, and Balthazar. The popular carol, "We Three Kings Of Orient Are," adds to this conclusion, but the Bible gives us no number and certainly no names for the wisemen.

When did the magi arrive in Bethlehem? It is common in Christmas pageants and in creches to have the angels, shepherds, and wisemen all at the manger at the same time. In point of fact, the Magi did not appear for at least forty-one days. How would we know that? Luke (in chapter 2) tells us that on the eighth day, in line with the Jewish law, Jesus was circumcised; and on the fortieth day, his parents took him to Jerusalem for the rite of purification and to present him to the Lord. "And they offered a sacrifice according to what is stated in the law of the Lord, 'a pair of turtledoves or two young pigeons'" (Luke 2:24).

The law in Leviticus, chapter 12, says that for the purification of the mother following the birth of a son, the sacrifice is to be a year-old lamb for a burnt offering and a pigeon or a turtledove for a sin offering. There is this added provision: "If she cannot afford a sheep, she shall take two turtledoves or two pigeons, one for a burnt offering and the other for a sin offering; and the priest shall make atonement on her behalf, and she shall be clean" (Leviticus 12:8). If the Magi had already arrived and given them gold, frankincense, and myrrh, Mary and Joseph could have afforded the lamb and the bird, and they would surely have done so.

It is also of note that the Magi came to Mary and her child in the house where they were staying. The time in the stable was past, the journey to Jerusalem had been made, and then the Magi's adoration of Jesus took place.

What is the rest — the aftermath — of the story?

King Herod was beyond enraged when he learned that the Magi had tricked him. Not knowing the identity of the child, Herod ordered the killing of all male children in and around Bethlehem who were two years old or under, according to the time he had learned from the wisemen. This does not necessarily mean that the Magi told him that the star appeared two years earlier. It does indicate that Herod wanted to be absolutely sure that he killed any rival to his throne. Such behavior was not uncharacteristic for Herod. He was a ruthless man and even executed a number of his own sons when he feared that they would usurp his throne.

For all that horror, Herod failed. Once again, before the innocent children of Bethlehem were killed, an angel of the Lord appeared to Joseph in a dream and told him to take Mary and Jesus and flee with them to Egypt. They remained there until after Herod died. The gifts from the Magi provided the resources that were required for this sojourn in Egypt.

Twice more, an angel appeared in dreams and instructed Joseph to return to Israel and then to go to the district of Galilee. The holy family settled in the town of Nazareth.

For thought or discussion:

- What fascinates you most about the story of the Magi?
- Why do you think people sometimes act in ways that are clearly evil?
- Have you ever experienced God's intervention that saved you from death or from harm?

(In church tradition, on liturgical calendars, and in religious art, Jesus' circumcision is known as The Name of Jesus [celebrated on January 1], the visit to the temple in Jerusalem is known as The Presentation of Our Lord [celebrated on February 2], the visit of the wisemen is known as The Epiphany [celebrated on January 6]; and the killing of the Bethlehem children is known as The Holy Innocents, Martyrs [celebrated on December 28].)

46. In My Father's House

Jesus at Twelve
Luke 2:41-52

The only childhood story about Jesus in Matthew, Mark, Luke, or John (other than those things that surrounded his birth, the flight into Egypt, and the return to Nazareth) is this account of the journey to Jerusalem for Passover when Jesus was twelve years old.

It was the family's custom to make the annual trek from Nazareth to Jerusalem for the celebration of Passover. In doing so, they were part of huge crowds of pilgrims, journeying from all over Israel to the temple in Jerusalem. They came to remember and to celebrate the deliverance of their ancestors from slavery in Egypt. Remembering the past, they also rejoiced in God's ongoing presence with his chosen people.

When the festival ended, Joseph and Mary set out with their family, friends, and host of other people traveling north. When it came time to settle down for the evening, Jesus was missing. Your first thought might be that Mary and Joseph were negligent parents. How could they have traveled a whole day and not checked up on their son? Or is it likely that Jesus, though only twelve years old, had been sufficiently responsible that his parents simply trusted him? And after all, the crowd included many relatives and friends.

It is interesting that Jesus was on the cusp of personal responsibility by Jewish standards. Bar Mitzvah (Bat Mitzvah for girls), occurring at the age of thirteen, is a coming of age ceremony for a Jewish boy. At this time he becomes a "son of the commandments" and is himself responsible for obeying Jewish law. While the institution of Bar Mitzvah was a later development in Judaism, the notion was surely present in Jesus' time that there came a point when a child was responsible for his actions and practices.

When Jesus' parents realized that he was not with the pilgrims, they hurried back to Jerusalem to find him. Here is the fear of every parent. Had they lost their son? What had happened to him? Would they ever find him? How could they have possibly lost this one?

Imagine the agonizing searching in Jerusalem. It was a large city with many sections, streets, and places to fascinate a boy. And what if he had been taken from the city by someone traveling to who knows where? Three days of searching must have felt like an eternity, and each hour that passed must have increased the sense of dread in Mary and Joseph.

Then they found Jesus. He was in the temple conversing with the teachers. He was asking questions, listening, and amazing these elders with his understanding. He was clearly engrossed in a most fascinating time of discussion and enlightenment.

His parents were beyond relieved when they found him, but they were also horrified at what might have been. Mary said, "Child, why have you treated us like this? Look, your father and I have been searching for you in great anxiety" (2:48). What an understated summary of their past three days.

Jesus' response must have been confounding to his parents. "Why were you searching for me? Did you not know that I must be in my Father's house?" (2:49). He must have seemed to them to be oblivious to their agony.

The three of them returned to Nazareth, and he "was obedient to them" (2:51). Jesus continued to grow in wisdom and in years; and Mary added this experience to the events on which she pondered: Gabriel's visit, the birth of Jesus, and the words that old Simeon spoke to her in the temple, "This child is destined for the falling and the rising of many in Israel, and to be a sign that will be opposed so that the inner thoughts of many will be revealed — and a sword will pierce your own soul too" (2:34-35).

For thought or discussion:

- Have you ever, even momentarily lost one of your children? What were your feelings?
- If you have ever been lost yourself, how would you describe that experience?
- What life experiences do you continue to ponder* as the years go by?

* Webster's Dictionary defines ponder as follows: to weigh in the mind; to think about; reflect on; to think or consider especially quietly, soberly, and deeply.

47. Forever Second Fiddle

John the Baptist
Matthew 3, 11, 14; Mark 1 and 6; Luke 1, 3, 7; John 1 and 3

He had a job of singular importance, but he was never going to be the star of the show.

Zechariah had been told by the angel Gabriel that his son's assignment would be to get the people ready for the Messiah to come. Before John was even conceived in his mother's womb, it was announced that he would live to point people to someone greater than himself.

John was to walk in the steps of the ancient prophet Elijah. He was (as mentioned earlier in chapter 41) to be a Nazirite, a sign person. He was to be filled with the Holy Spirit. He was to wait in the wilderness until it was time to begin his ministry. He was a loner, but he may have spent time with the Essenes.

When the time was right, John began to declare, "Repent, for the kingdom of heaven has come near" (Matthew 3:2). Clothed in camel's hair, sustained on locusts and wild honey, and girded with a leather belt, he proclaimed a baptism of repentance, saying, "The one who is more powerful than I is coming after me; I am not worthy to stoop down and untie the thong of his sandals. I have baptized you with water; but he will baptize you with the Holy Spirit" (Mark 1:7-8).

The people thronged to John as he preached beside the Jordan River. They were captivated by his call to repentance and to right living. They were baptized by him in the river as a sign that they had heard his call and were to be numbered among those who were prepared for the Messiah to come. His fame spread, and he could have parlayed that into stardom.

The religious leaders from Jerusalem asked him who he was and what his credentials were for what he was doing. John said he was neither the Messiah nor the prophet Elijah. Instead, he declared, "I am the voice of one crying out in the wilderness, 'Make straight the way of the Lord'" (John 1:23). In saying this, he identified himself with the Old Testament prophet Isaiah (cf. Isaiah 40:3), and again he announced the coming of the Messiah.

Among those who came to be baptized by John was Jesus. "John would have prevented him, saying, 'I need to be baptized by you, and do you come to me?' But Jesus answered him, 'Let it be so now; for it is proper for us in this way to fulfill all righteousness'" (Matthew 3:14-15).

That baptism was unlike any other that John performed. When Jesus came up out of the water, "the heaven was opened, and the Holy Spirit descended upon him in bodily form like a dove. And a voice came from heaven, 'You are my Son, the Beloved; with you I am well pleased'" (Luke 3:21-22). This was the one whose way John had been sent to prepare.

Later, John declared, "the one who sent me to baptize with water said to me 'He on whom you see the Spirit descend and remain is the one who baptizes with the Holy Spirit.' And I myself have seen and have testified that this is the Son of God" (John 1:33-34).

When it was brought to John's attention that many of his former followers were leaving him to follow Jesus, he responded, "He who has the bride is the bridegroom. The friend of the bridegroom, who stands and hears him, rejoices greatly at the bridegroom's voice. For this reason, my joy has been fulfilled. He must increase, but I must decrease" (John 3:29-30).

John the Baptist was a man who spoke the truth and was not shy about doing so. It caused him to clearly point to Jesus as the one to be followed. It also led to his death at the hands of King Herod. When Herod married Herodias, his brother Philip's wife, John declared that it was unlawful. He said it loudly and frequently. It cost him his head (Cf. Mark 6:14-29).

John the Baptist had a job of singular importance, but he was never the star of the show.

For thought or discussion:

- Have you ever had an important job that was designed to put someone else in the spotlight?
- Have you ever been in a position where it pleased you to be second best?
- Have you ever had an experience where it galled you to be regarded as second best?

(In church tradition and on liturgical calendars, The Baptism of Our Lord is celebrated early in January on the first Sunday following The Epiphany. The liturgical color is white.)

48. If You Are the Son of God . . .

The Temptation of Jesus
Matthew 4, Mark 1, Luke 4

"If" is a small word that implies a challenge, and it often conveys negativity. That is how it was when Jesus and Satan contended in the wilderness.

Following Jesus' baptism, he was driven into the wilderness by the Holy Spirit. There he was for forty days, and during that time he fasted.

Temptations come most easily at points of weakness, need, vulnerability, or pride.

"If you are the Son of God," Satan said to Jesus, "command these stones to become loaves of bread" (Matthew 4:3). The tempter, calling into question Jesus' identity, challenged him to do that which should be child's play for the very Son of the One who created all that exists. Here was an easy way for Jesus to demonstrate his power and to provide a most basic human necessity, food to sustain the body. Here was a chance to do something meaningful and practical. Hunger can drive one to extreme measures, and proving one's ability and character can be a powerful motivator.

Jesus, however, answered, "It is written, 'One does not live by bread alone, but by every word that comes from the mouth of God'" (Matthew 4:4.) Jesus responded by quoting the Scriptures to Satan. He did not need to make up a new and catchy phrase to win this round. He leaned on God's word to speak the truth and to ward off the tempter's attack. There are things more important than satisfying physical hunger. Jesus had no need to prove his power to Satan.

Satan, of course, was not easily deterred. Where one temptation failed to win the day, he had more tricks in his toolbox.

You will note that while Mark gives no details about any actual temptations, Matthew and Luke record the same three. The second and third temptations are in reverse order in Matthew and Luke, but they are the same two temptations.

The devil, in an instant, placed before Jesus all the kingdoms of the world. Cunningly, the tempter said, "To you I will give their glory and all this authority; for it has been given over to me, and I give it to anyone I please. If you, then, will worship me, it will all be yours" (Luke 4:6-7). The prince of liars spoke according to his nature. For the price of Jesus' soul, Satan promised to give that which he did not in fact possess. The world and its people and nations did not belong to him, but that didn't stop him from dangling before Jesus the thought of all the good a person could do if he ruled the world. The temptation was to have absolute power, and the requirement was to worship Satan. Jesus well knew that only God had absolute power and that the devil was promising what he neither had nor could deliver. Once again, Jesus responded by quoting God's word to the devil. "It is written, 'Worship the Lord your God, and serve only him'" (Luke 4:8).

Taking Jesus to Jerusalem and placing him on the pinnacle of the temple, Satan tried yet another ploy. This time, Satan himself quoted Scripture to Jesus. "If you are the Son of God, throw yourself down from here, for it is written, 'He will command his angels concerning you, to protect you,' and 'On their hands they will bear you up, so that you will not dash your foot against a stone'" (Luke 4:9-11). The third temptation was to do something spectacular, for people are easily awed and swayed by the spectacular. After all, what better way to show that you are God's Son than to rally the angels to your defense. This temptation was also a challenge to Jesus to prove that he trusted his heavenly Father to save him from harm.

Jesus' response was this word from the sixth chapter of Deuteronomy: "Do not put the Lord your God to the test."

Jesus came for a far higher purpose than to change stones into bread, to have temporal rule of all the kingdoms and nations of the earth, or to wow the crowds with spectacular tricks. He came to do nothing less than to conquer sin, death, and the power of the devil. Where darkness, hatred, weakness, shame, and death prevailed, Jesus came to bring light, love, strength, forgiveness, and life. Jesus' eyes were so clearly focused on God that Satan could not turn him from his purpose to set all things right again.

Matthew and Mark relate that when Satan departed, angels came and ministered to Jesus. And Luke writes, "When the devil had finished every test, he departed from him until an opportune time" (4:13). Evil and temptation do not go away; they hide in the darkness until a new opportunity presents itself.

For thought or discussion:

- When Satan comes calling, what temptation does he most often place before you?
- How does knowing that Jesus overcame the tempter's ploys encourage you as you live your life?
- Are there other stories or passages of the Bible that help you resist temptations?

49. First Things First

Healing the Paralytic
Mark 2

(Matthew 9 and Luke 5)

Jesus began his public ministry by declaring, "The time is fulfilled, and the kingdom of God has come near; repent and believe in the good news" (Mark 1:15). His healings, exorcisms, miracles, and teachings all pointed to the truth of that proclamation.

One day, in the town of Capernaum, a crowd came to hear what Jesus had to say. The people had heard about him, and so they completely filled the house and gathered around the door, wanting to listen to him. There was probably the expectation that he would also heal some people as he had been doing throughout Galilee.

With just that thought in mind, four men came carrying a paralyzed man on a mat of some sort. The crowd was so dense that they were unable to get to Jesus, but they had come for a purpose, and they did not intend to go home without at least bringing their friend to Jesus. Desperate times called for desperate measures.

They climbed up on the flat roof of the house and hauled up their friend on his mat. Then to get access to Jesus, they began to take up the roof tiles, no doubt causing dust and dirt to fall on and irritate the people below. Then sunlight began to fill the room, attention was diverted from Jesus, and all eyes were turned upward. When the opening was large enough, the men lowered their friend into the midst of the crowd.

When Jesus saw the faith of the four men, made evident by their efforts, he said to the man who was paralyzed, "Son, your sins are forgiven" (2:5). That set the room buzzing! While many of the people were still trying to figure out what was happening, the religious leaders who were present were scandalized. "It is blasphemy!" they said, "Who can forgive sins but God alone?" (2:7). The four men on the roof were confused, disappointed, and maybe even angry; for they had come to get their friend healed.

Jesus raised the question, "Which is easier, to say to the paralytic, 'Your sins are forgiven,' or to say, 'Stand up and take your mat and walk'?" (2:9). On the one hand, the answer would be the former, since there would be no visible proof of Jesus' power to forgive sins, while it would be clearly visible if the man could walk or not. On the other hand, it is true that the power to forgive sins belongs to God while the ability to heal is often given to humans.

Cutting to the chase, Jesus said, "'But so that you may know that the Son of Man has authority on earth to forgive sins' — he said to the paralytic — 'I say to you, stand up, take your mat and go to your home'" (2:10-11). And immediately the man stood up, picked up his mat, and walked out. His friends scrambled off the roof and ran after him, and the crowd was amazed and praised God, saying, "We have never seen anything like this!" (2:12).

With Jesus, it was first things first. The adage is, "When you have your health, you have everything." Jesus, however, knew that a person who is physically healthy but living in unforgiven sin, is trapped in inner turmoil. A person whose sins are forgiven and who therefore lives in harmony with God, is free and can be at peace even when physically less than whole. From the beginning, God's desire for the world was that all people should live in harmony, peace, and health. Since it is sin that destroys harmony and peace, forgiveness is the first and most important thing.

For thought or discussion:

- What extremes have you undergone to bring healing to yourself or to someone you love?
- Has there been a time when illness, physical pain, or suffering brought you closer to God?
- Have you experienced the freeing power of forgiveness?

50. Chosen to Change the World

Selecting the Disciples
Mark 3

(Matthew 10 and Luke 6)

Jesus came to redeem the world, and this was a one-man job. To get this good news to every corner of the globe, however, was to be done by an ever-growing host of people who had come to know this truth. To accomplish this task would require an initial core group who would witness what Jesus did and begin to make it known.

If you were to assemble such a group of people, what qualifications would you be hoping to find? You would surely want some people who were eloquent, some who had organizational skills and imagination, some who were good recruiters, and certainly some money people. You would want people who could think outside the box. You would want your team to be educated, wise, and learned in the ways of the people and culture in which they lived. You would want people who enjoyed traveling and engaging people of other languages and cultures and who were at least bilingual. It would be helpful if your people were both bold and sensitive. If some of your team members were well connected with people of means and power, that would be a definite plus. Today, of course, you would want people who were very tech-savvy. You would want people who had experience in planning, development, and community organizing.

Who did Jesus choose and what were their qualifications?

Mark tells us that Jesus "appointed twelve, whom he also named apostles, to be with him, and to be sent out to proclaim the message, and to have authority to cast out demons…Simon (to whom he gave the name Peter); James son of Zebedee and John the brother of James (to whom he gave the name…Sons of Thunder); and Andrew, and Philip, and Bartholomew, and Matthew, and Thomas, and James son of Alphaeus, and Thaddeus, and Simon the Cananaean, and Judas Iscariot, who betrayed him" (3:14-19).

Of all the people who were drawn to Jesus, why did he choose these twelve? At least three of them were fishermen, one was a tax collector; and the Bible tells us nothing about the professions of the other eight. Simon the Cananaean was identified as a Zealot, but that was not his occupation. We will discover that Peter, James, and John were apparently singled out among the twelve for some special times with Jesus, that Peter seems to have been often the boldest, and that Thomas was one who demanded proof and raised questions.

Fishermen had to be skilled at their trade and to know something about marketing their catch. A tax collector would have known about money, accounting, and writing. A Zealot would have had enthusiasm for the traditions of Israel and for the task at hand. A person who asks questions is always beneficial to have on a team. But where were the letters of recommendation, the certificates, the diplomas, and the designations of honor and of accomplishment? By the world's standards, these twelve were quite ordinary men, but Jesus saw their hearts and chose them. (This is even true of Judas Iscariot who was to betray Jesus — a story yet to be told.) Often it is the "common people" who are the backbone of any important enterprise, for when all is said and done, they prove to be loyal, dependable, diligent, and wise beyond expectation.

Jesus likely chose twelve men to correspond to the twelve tribes of Israel (and in eastern numerology, twelve is a complete number). The fact that all were men was not an indication of Jesus' preference for men over women but rather the simple reality that in his day, the testimony of women was not regarded as trustworthy. (We will have more to say about that in a later, climactic story.) The success of the mission depended on getting an initial hearing from the populace.

Most of these original disciples experienced less than pleasant deaths, but they willingly gave all they had for their Master. While these chosen twelve frequently seemed to struggle to understand what Jesus did or said, there is no doubting the success of that for which they lived and died; for the good news of Jesus has indeed been spread all around the globe.

For thought or discussion:

- What do you think are the most important qualifications when choosing volunteers?
- Have you ever been asked to take on a task that took you out of your comfort zone?
- Recount a time when such an experience caused you positive growth and satisfaction.

51. The Sign of the Wine

The Wedding at Cana
John 2

A wedding is intended to be a joyous occasion as a man and a woman confirm their love for each other and promise to live as husband and wife "'til death do us part." Weddings are filled with delight and passion in the present and with unbounded hope for the future. Weddings and funerals are two occasions when extended families make every effort to gather, and weddings are usually the happier of the two events. Weddings are absolutely worth celebrating in style.

So it was that a particular wedding took place in the town of Cana in Galilee, and Jesus and his disciples were invited guests. Jesus' mother, Mary, was also a guest at the wedding of this unnamed couple.

There is a great deal of planning that goes into preparing for a wedding. Who will be the witnesses, and how big will the wedding party be? What colors will be used? What about a dress and a cake? Plans need to be made for the wedding service itself, such as the place, officiant, music, flowers, and the wording of the service. By far the greatest stress is connected to making sure that everything is ready for the reception or party that follows the ceremony, whether it lasts for a few hours or for a day or more. Will the location be beautiful enough, and what sort of decorations will be required? Will the weather cooperate? Will there be music, and who will provide it? Will there be hors d'oeuvres, and if so, what variety? Where will each guest be seated to be sure that each person has the best experience possible? What will be served?

The greatest fear for the bride and groom and for the parents of each is that there will not be enough food and drinks to satisfy all the guests. At the wedding in Cana, one of those fears became real. There was not enough wine for the guests. This was a genuine crisis for those hosting the wedding reception.

Mary had an easy solution. She told her son, confident that he could solve the dilemma. His response to her, however, was, "Woman, what concern is that to you and to me? My hour has not yet come" (2:4). But she, undeterred by his response, and in wonderful motherly fashion, told the servants, "Do whatever he tells you" (2:5). The ball was back in Jesus' court.

There were six stone jars, each holding twenty or thirty gallons, for the Jewish purification rites. Jesus told the servants to fill them all with water. When they had done that, he directed them to draw some out and to take it to the steward of the feast (the man in charge of the festivities). This man was not about to serve any wine without being sure that it was at least passable. To his surprise, this wine was superior. He told the bridegroom that he was amazed that the very best wine had been saved until the end. Somewhere between one hundred twenty and one hundred eighty gallons of excellent wine were provided, and embarrassment for the bridegroom was averted.

"Jesus did this, the first of his signs, in Cana of Galilee, and revealed his glory; and his disciples believed in him" (2:11). Changing water into wine was certainly amazing, but how is it that doing so revealed Jesus' glory or caused his disciples to believe in him? It doesn't say that they believed that he could do awesome things. It says that they believed in him.

Perhaps the answer is in the apocalyptic literature and teachings of the centuries leading up to the coming of Jesus. In these traditions, many signs were put forth as indications of the arrival of the Messiah and the coming of the kingdom of God. There were clues for which to be on the alert. One such image or clue related to wine.

It was said that when God's glorious kingdom came, the earth would be so fruitful, that a single grape vine would have thousands of branches, that each branch would have thousands of twigs, that each twig would have thousands of shoots, that each shoot would have thousands of clusters, that each cluster would have thousands of grapes, and that each grape would produce a couple hundred gallons of wine.

What Jesus did at the wedding in Cana was not as grand as that apocalyptic vision, but it was clearly far more wine than the occasion required. And even though the transformation of water to wine was observed only by the disciples and the servants (and possibly Mary), this miracle was more than enough to cause the disciples to believe in Jesus.

For thought or discussion:

- Have you ever had a party that threatened to unravel because of the scarcity of food or drink?
- Has there been a time when God provided resources for you in a time of need?
- What sign has caused you to believe in Jesus and in the kingdom of God?

52. Words for Living

The Sermon on the Mount
Matthew 5-7

One day, as crowds of people gathered around Jesus, he sat down and began to teach them what it meant to live as God intended people to live. What he said was not what would normally be expected in a world where the power of Rome seemed to set the standard. For the "common people," striving to gain power of their own and to have freedom from the oppression that marked so many of their days, the words Jesus spoke were equally surprising.

He began this way: "Blessed are the poor in spirit…those who mourn…the meek…those who hunger and thirst for righteousness…the merciful…the pure in heart…the peacemakers…," (5:3-9) and then he added, "Blessed are those who are persecuted for righteousness' sake…Blessed are you when people revile you and persecute you and utter all kinds of evil against you falsely on my account. Rejoice and be glad, for your reward is great in heaven, for in the same way they persecuted the prophets who were before you" (5:10-12). (Verses 3-12 are called the Beatitudes.)

The people may have wondered if Jesus was telling them to suffer patiently. Was he trying to make them feel somewhat better about their ordinary (and sometimes impoverished) lives? The longer they listened to him, however, the more they began to realize that he was calling them to be aggressively active in living purposeful lives of godly goodness.

He declared that the people listening to him were the salt of the earth and the light of the world. He announced that he had come to fulfill the law and the prophets. He explained the radical difference between fulfilling the spirit of God's law instead of simply settling for the letter of the law. He called them to "Love your enemies and pray for those who persecute you" (5:44) and to "Be perfect, therefore, as your heavenly Father is perfect" (5:48). These were all words of action.

Jesus urged his hearers to do all that God's law required but not to do it in a showy way to impress other people. Whether giving alms, or praying, or fasting, each practice was to be done only to glorify God. In place of long and elaborate prayer, Jesus gave the people the perfect model for all prayer, that which became known as The Lord's Prayer (6:9-13).

He spoke about the dangers of trusting in worldly treasures and the futility of the worrying that consumes people. "So do not worry about tomorrow, for tomorrow will bring worries of its own. Today's trouble is enough for today" (6:34).

Jesus challenged the people to seek God's guidance in making right judgments in life but to refrain from living with judgmental attitudes. Instead, he told them to actively seek the good of all people, saying, "In everything do to others as you would have them do to you" (7:12) We have come to know this as the Golden Rule.

"Ask, and it will be given you; search, and you will find; knock, and the door will be opened for you," (7:7) he said. In saying this, he reminded the people of God's infinite goodness and love. Jesus called his hearers to be agents of such love and grace, actively transforming their world.

Jesus ended this "Sermon on the Mount" with the image of two men who each built a house. One built on solid rock, and the other built on sand. When the floods came, the former stood firm, but the latter house fell in ruins. "Everyone then who hears these words of mine and acts on them," Jesus said, "will be like a wise man who built his house on rock" (7:24).

When Jesus finished his teaching, the people were astonished "for he taught them as one having authority, and not as their scribes" (7:29). The scribes normally taught by quoting other learned scribes, believing that the words of previous teachers gave credibility to their own teaching. Jesus' authority, by contrast, was God-given, spoken from his own heart. The challenge to his hearers was profound as he called them to live lives of radical and powerful love.

For thought or discussion:

- When have you listened to a speaker who captured your imagination and altered your thinking?
- Share a teaching that frequently comes to mind as you travel your journey of life.
- What does it mean to you to be "the salt of the earth" or "the light of the world"?

53. To Raise the Dead

The Widow's Son at Nain
Luke 7

Life is marked both by surprising joy and wonder and also by crushing defeat and loss.

She was a woman who had likely experienced joy and wonder in her marriage and in the birth of her son. She had also experienced the death of her husband, which meant she was dependent on her son for security as the remaining years of her life unfolded. How reassuring it was to have one on whom she could depend. It did not erase her grief as she remembered her husband, but it did give her confidence and hope as she lived into the future.

Then her son died. Like Ruth in the Old Testament, this woman was bereft of both husband and son. Unlike Ruth, there is no indication that she had a daughter-in-law to give support or comfort. She was alone.

The people of Nain who knew her, surely rallied around her. People do that at the time of a death. It is altogether likely that food was brought to her home along with words and signs of condolence. Some of those who came probably spoke too many words, and there were other times when either awkward or welcome silence prevailed. Grieving is, when all is said and done, a solitary business.

The day arrived for the burial of this widow's only son. A large crowd from the town accompanied the widow and those who carried the man's body. She wept, and likely there were few dry eyes among those in that sad procession. Funerals and burials can be such wrenching events of finality.

It happened that Jesus, followed by his disciples and a large crowd, approached the town of Nain at just that moment. Seeing the widow, he was moved with compassion; and he said to her, "Do not weep" (7:13). How could she not weep? Did he have no understanding of the depth of her loss?

Jesus understood fully. He was not a man who spoke careless words or offered meaningless platitudes. Jesus always backed up his words with his actions. He walked forward and touched the bier on which the body was being carried. Those who carried it stopped. Jesus said, "Young man, I say to you, rise!" (7:14). At that, the formerly dead man sat up and began to speak. Jesus restored him to life and gave him back to his amazed and grateful mother.

As for the crowds of people, "Fear seized all of them; and they glorified God, saying 'A great prophet has risen among us!' and 'God has looked favorably on his people!'" (7:16). This was certainly the talk of the town and a story that was told and retold in Nain, the surrounding countryside, and throughout Judea. It was another sign to point to Jesus' true identity and purpose.

For thought or discussion:

- When have you experienced the death of someone dear to you?
- What brought you comfort at that time?
- How have you been able to bring comfort to someone else who was grieving?

54. Calm Amidst the Raging Storm

Stilling the Storm
Mark 4

(Matthew 8, Luke 8)

On one occasion, Jesus was teaching beside the Sea of Galilee. The crowd was so large that he got into a boat and sat there to teach as the people gathered on the beach.

When evening came and darkness began to descend, Jesus directed his disciples to join him in the boat so that they could cross to the other side of the lake.

As they sailed along, a windstorm swept down on the water. Sudden storms were not uncommon, but this particular storm was severe. Some of the disciples were fishermen and very much at home on the lake; but even they became fearful as the waves rose higher and higher, and breaking over the gunwales of their boat threatened to sink their vessel.

As the boat pitched and rolled, Jesus calmly slept on a cushion in the stern. He was likely weary from the events of the day, and he seemed oblivious to the increasing anxiety of the disciples and the worsening of the storm.

With their fear bordering on panic, the disciples woke Jesus saying, "Teacher, do you not care that we are perishing?" (4:38).

Jesus woke up, rebuked the wind, and said to the sea, "Peace! Be still!" (4:39) and there was a dead calm. He then asked his incredulous disciples why they had been afraid and why they had so little faith. He stilled the storm on the sea. He desired also to still the storms in their hearts and minds.

They may have been surprised by his questions, but they were absolutely amazed by what had taken place. They said among themselves, "Who then is this, that even the wind and the sea obey him?" (4:41).

Who indeed was this Jesus who had power not only over illnesses and diseases but also over nature itself? How could he, with just a word, do such powerful things?

For thought or discussion:

- What storms rage in your life and cause you to be afraid?
- Does Jesus at times seem to be asleep and unconcerned with what is troubling you?
- Have you been comforted by knowing that Jesus sails your life with you?

55. Legion and the Swine

The Gerasene Demoniac
Mark 5

(Matthew 8 and Luke 8)

Imagine being accosted by a deranged person. The unsettling situation is fraught with unpredictability. The first thought is to get away as far and as quickly as possible, for anything done or said might have a devastating effect.

Jesus and his disciples sailed across the Sea of Galilee and landed on the eastern shore in the region of the Decapolis (the ten cities). When they came ashore, they were immediately met by a demon-possessed man who ran up to Jesus and bowed before him. Jesus commanded the unclean spirit to come out of the man. At this, the man yelled at the top of his lungs, "What have you to do with me, Jesus, Son of the Most High God? I adjure you by God, do not torment me" (5:7).

This man had been living among the tombs in the cemetery. Day and night, he howled in the cemetery and on the surrounding hills. He bruised himself with stones, and he terrified the people of the region. Sometimes he was clothed, and other times he ran around naked. Attempts had repeatedly and unsuccessfully been made to restrain this man with chains and with shackles. He broke the shackles and wrenched apart the chains. He was wild; he was strong; he was a terror!

Jesus asked the man for his name. "He replied, 'My name is Legion; for we are many'" (5:9). Then the demons, who clearly knew who Jesus was, begged him not to send them out of the country. Noticing a herd of pigs feeding on a nearby hill, they asked to be sent into the swine. At Jesus' command, the unclean spirits came out of Legion; and with Jesus' permission, the demons entered into the pigs. This was great news for the man but terrible news for the pigs and their owners. Inhabited by the unclean spirits, the swine, numbering about two thousand, rushed down the hill into the Sea of Galilee and were drowned.

The swineherds ran off and told what had happened, needing to explain how they had lost the pigs that had been left in their care. The people of the region, receiving this news, came to see for themselves what had happened.

They found Jesus and the man sitting together. The man was fully clothed and in his right mind. Rather than rejoicing in the exorcism that freed and reclaimed this man, the people were afraid and begged Jesus to leave their area. Although the exorcism was indeed awesome, if such restorations came at the cost of herds of pigs, having Jesus around would prove to have a negative impact on their economy. Which was more to be desired, safe herds with a demon-possessed man, or a man made whole at any cost?

As Jesus prepared to leave the area, the man wanted to go with him. "But Jesus refused, and said to him, 'Go home to your friends, and tell them how much the Lord has done for you, and what mercy he has shown you'" (5:19). And throughout the region of the Decapolis, that is exactly what the man did; and people were amazed.

For thought or discussion:

- Have you ever been around someone who seemed out of control and therefore made you afraid?
- What do you consider more important, the wellbeing of individuals or the financial bottom line?
- What life-altering experience have you had, and with whom have you shared it?

56. Life Restored
Jairus' Daughter and the Bleeding Woman
Mark 5

(Matthew 9 and Luke 8)

Life is filled with interruptions, and oftentimes life is defined by those interruptions. What is true of life is also true of ministry, for in the midst of plans and agendas, the needs of others break in and call for attention.

Jesus and his disciples returned from the land of the Gerasenes and the encounter with Legion. Crowds gathered around them when they came ashore. Two of the people in the crowd were in special need of Jesus' ministry that day.

Jairus, a leader of the synagogue, fell on his knees at Jesus' feet and begged him, "My little daughter is at the point of death. Come and lay your hands on her, so that she may be made well, and live" (5:23). Whatever plans Jesus may have had, he went with Jairus, for this was surely an urgent mission. The crowds followed along and pressed in on Jesus.

In that crowd was a woman who had been suffering with hemorrhages for twelve years. She had gone from doctor to doctor and spent all that she had, but she was no better. In fact, she grew worse, and she was desperate. She worked her way through the crowd until she was close enough to Jesus to touch his cloak, "for she said, 'If I but touch his clothes, I will be made well'" (5:28). When she touched Jesus' cloak, she immediately felt in her body that her hemorrhage had ceased and that she was healed. Just a touch was all it took, and who but she alone would be the wiser?

Jesus knew. Sensing that power had gone forth from him, he turned to the crowd and asked, "Who touched my clothes?" (5:30). The disciples were surprised and dismissive. In a crowd there is always some jostling and touching. But Jesus knew that this was something else entirely, and so did the woman. She came forward, trembling and fearful, and told him the truth of what she had done. "He said to her, 'Daughter, your faith has made you well; go in peace, and be healed of your disease'" (5:34). Interrupted on his mission of mercy, Jesus healed her.

Time is often of the essence when life and death are on the line. So it was that some people came to break the news to Jairus that his twelve-year-old daughter had died and that there was no need to trouble Jesus any further. Hearing this, Jesus said to Jairus, "Do not fear, only believe" (5:36).

Leaving the crowd behind, and taking only Peter, James, and John, Jesus went with Jairus to his home. There they encountered a group of people weeping and wailing, grieving the girl's death. Jesus said, "Why do you make a commotion and weep? The child is not dead but sleeping" (5:39). They all laughed at Jesus, for they knew death when they saw it. Taking only the parents and his disciples with him, Jesus went into the room where the girl was. Taking her by the hand, he said to her, "Little girl, get up!" (5:41). She did so immediately and began to walk around. He told her parents to give her something to eat. He also told the amazed parents not to share this news.

Such an injunction to silence often followed Jesus' life-renewing actions. The reason for the injunction was not reverse psychology, but rather the need for the people to take time to reflect deeply on what had been done for them. Only then would the message that they proclaimed be focused on the giver of the gift rather than simply on the gift itself.

A woman was restored to health after twelve years of suffering. A twelve-year-old girl was restored to life. The future was opened for both of them; disease and death were interrupted.

For thought or discussion:

- When has an interruption in your schedule become the most important event of the day?
- Have you had a prolonged illness that has tried your patience and left you weary?
- Have you experienced a healing that has been unexpected and that has felt miraculous?

57. Under Cover of Darkness

Nicodemus
John 3

Nicodemus was a respected man, a Pharisee, and a Jewish religious leader. He was also fascinated by what he was hearing about Jesus, and he wanted to know more about him. Since Jesus was regarded with suspicion or disapproval by most of the religious leaders, this created a problem for Nicodemus. He did what people usually do when they want to explore a forbidden subject; he went secretly by night to meet Jesus.

Nicodemus addressed Jesus in a most positive and respectful way. "Rabbi, we know that you are a teacher who has come from God; for no one can do these signs that you do apart from the presence of God" (3:2). Unstated is the question, *Who are you, really?* Coming under cover of darkness, Nicodemus wanted to be convinced that Jesus was worth following openly in the light of day.

As frequently happened when people talked with Jesus, the conversation took an unexpected turn. "Very truly, I tell you," Jesus said, "no one can see the kingdom of God without being born from above [or born anew]" (3:3). Perplexed, Nicodemus responded, "How can anyone be born after having grown old? Can one enter a second time into the mother's womb and be born?" (3:4). Whatever did that mean? And imagine what a horror it would be to any mother, if such a thing were necessary for anyone to see the kingdom of God.

Jesus continued, "Very truly, I tell you, no one can enter the kingdom of God without being born of water and Spirit. What is born of the flesh is flesh, and what is born of the Spirit is spirit." (3:5-6). This did not clear things up for Nicodemus. He must have stood there shaking his head. "How can these things be?" (3:9).

What Jesus said in answer to this question likely set Nicodemus' head spinning. Jesus told Nicodemus that "just as Moses lifted up the serpent in the wilderness, so must the Son of Man be lifted up, that whoever believes in him may have eternal life. For God so loved the world that he gave his only Son, so that everyone who believes in him may not perish but may have eternal life" (3:14-16). Jesus called Nicodemus to remember his scriptures, specifically chapter 21 of Numbers. During Israel's passage from Egypt to the promised land, the peoples' rebellion resulted in venomous serpents biting and killing many of the Israelites. When they called for God's mercy, Moses was directed to make a bronze serpent and raise it on a pole, so that any who had been bitten, but looked on it, would live.

What was Nicodemus to make of this? Then Jesus added, "Those who believe in [the Son] are not condemned; but those who do not believe are condemned already, because they have not believed in the name of the only Son of God. And this is the judgment, that the light has come into the world, and people loved darkness rather than light because their deeds were evil" (3:18-19). It would be hard to miss the assertion that, in Jesus, Nicodemus was dealing with far more than merely a teacher who had come from God. Jesus challenged Nicodemus to vastly expand his expectations and to imagine the unimaginable: "For God so loved the world that he gave his only Son…"

Nicodemus left this nighttime meeting with Jesus, still groping in the dark in terms of understanding; but what he had heard and experienced percolated in his mind. In the end, he was very willing to be with Jesus in the light of day. Stay tuned.

For thought or discussion:

- Have you ever secretly checked out a person to understand him or her better?
- John 3:16 is one of the most familiar verses in the Bible. How do you understand it?
- Do Jesus' sayings every cause you confusion?

58. Perfectly Known

The Woman at the Well
John 4

It all began with a simple request for a drink of water. Well, it wasn't quite as simple as it might have seemed, for the request was made to a Samaritan woman by a Jewish man.

When the Assyrians destroyed the northern kingdom, they scattered the Israelites throughout their realm and resettled Samaria (the northern kingdom territory) with a variety of peoples from other parts of their kingdom. The Samaritans, therefore, became a mixed race and were considered impure or unclean by the Jews. Samaritans were to be avoided and were not to be trusted. For a Jewish man to speak to a strange woman was also considered improper, so the simple request crossed a number of serious social boundaries.

Jesus and his disciples were walking from Judea to Galilee, and they had to go through Samaria. This brought them to Sychar, a city near the location of a well that the patriarch Jacob had dug. While the disciples went into the city to buy food, Jesus, tired from the journey, sat down beside the well.

At about noon, the Samaritan woman came to draw water. The fact that she came at noon could have been because she was off her schedule that day, for normally such a chore would have been done first thing in the morning or in the cool of the evening. It is likely that the timing had more to do with her standing in the community. As you will discover shortly, this woman may not have been a favorite among the women of Sychar. She may well have chosen to come at an unusual time to avoid the whispers and sidelong glances of the other women. So here she was in the heat of the day to draw the water she needed.

Jesus made his request. Understandably, her first response was to ask why he, a Jewish man, was speaking to her. Jesus' response did not answer her question. He said, "If you knew the gift of God, and who it is that is saying to you, 'Give me a drink,' you would have asked him, and he would have given you living water" (4:10). She, clearly puzzled, wondered how he who had no bucket was going to draw water for her. She asked him how he planned to get that living water; and she asked him also if he was greater than their ancestor Jacob, who had dug the well.

Once again, rather than answering those specific questions, Jesus continued, "Everyone who drinks of this water will be thirsty again, but those who drink of the water that I will give them will never be thirsty. The water that I will give will become in them a spring of water gushing up to eternal life" (4:13-14). That sounded like a winning idea to the woman — to never be thirsty and to no longer need to come to the well to draw water.

That was the beginning of the conversation, but it was hardly the end of it. Jesus told the woman to go and get her husband and come back with him. She replied that she was not married. Jesus agreed, rightly saying that she had been married and divorced five times and was currently living with a man who was not her husband.* How did he know this about her? She must have been surprised and perhaps embarrassed, so she changed the subject.

"Sir, I see that you are a prophet. Our ancestors worshiped on this mountain, but you say that the place where people must worship is in Jerusalem" (4:19-20). Actually, Jesus had said nothing about that, but it moved the conversation away from her personal life.

Jesus, however, did not shy away from the new topic. He told her that ultimately the specific location of worship was not the point. He said, "But the hour is coming, and is now here, when the true worshipers will worship the Father in spirit and truth" (4:23). She responded by saying that she knew the Messiah would be coming, and that he would clear up all these things. To this, Jesus responded, "I am he, the one who is speaking to you" (4:26).

At that point, the disciples returned, amazed to find Jesus talking to the woman. They didn't dare openly question Jesus, but they certainly wondered why he was engaged in this conversation.

The woman, on the other hand, leaving her water jar behind, hurried back to the city and breathlessly said to the people, "Come and see a man who told me everything I have ever done! He cannot be the Messiah, can he?" (4:29).

Many of the people came with her to meet Jesus, and they believed in him because of what the woman had said. They urged Jesus and his disciples to stay with them, and they did so for two days.

When Jesus and his disciples left Sychar, he left behind many believers who said to the woman, "It is no longer because of what you said that we believe, for we have heard for ourselves, and we know that this is truly the Savior of the world" (4:42).

A simple request for a drink of water became the fountain of faith for many people.

For thought or discussion:

- Have you ever been embarrassed in a conversation and wanted to change the subject?
- Have you ever had a conversation with someone who seemed to deeply know you immediately?
- Which of Jesus' words or sayings make you feel uncomfortable, and which bring you peace?

* Every indication is that this woman was both intelligent and learned. Only a man could divorce his wife, so she had been rejected five times. Was this because her intelligence threatened her husbands? The cause of divorce could not have been adultery, or she would almost certainly have been put to death by stoning.

59. A Banquet Prepared

Feeding the Five Thousand
Mark 6

(Matthew 14, Luke 9, John 6)

Jesus had a way of drawing a crowd. When he came into a region, word spread like wildfire. People who had either seen him or heard about him flocked to him to hear his teaching and to ask for healing. Even when Jesus wanted some time alone or some private teaching time with his disciples, likely as not, a crowd would gather.

Because these gatherings were not scheduled ahead of time, but happened spontaneously, preparations were not made in advance for food or drinks or anything else. As groups of people passed through towns and villages looking for Jesus, other curious people dropped whatever they were doing and joined the throng to find him.

On one such occasion, Jesus and his disciples had sailed across the Sea of Galilee to find a deserted place where they could rest and recharge. As they came ashore, a crowd had already gathered. Jesus "had compassion for them, because they were like sheep without a shepherd; and he began to teach them many things" (6:34). Because he had much to say, and because the people hung on his words, the time passed quickly until the day was far advanced.

Concerned, the disciples came to Jesus and urged him to dismiss the crowd so that the people could go into neighboring towns and find food for themselves. No doubt the disciples were also hungry by this time, and they assumed that Jesus was as well.

Jesus had another idea. He said, "You give them something to eat" (6:37). Their immediate response was a bit of panic. To feed such a crowd would cost half a year's wages, they said — surely a most impractical notion. Jesus asked them how much food they had. Taking inventory of their provisions didn't take long at all. "There is a boy here who has five barley loaves and two fish. But what are they among so many people?" (John 6:9).

A glance at the food and a glance at the crowd was all they needed to be convinced of scarcity.

Jesus, on the other hand, saw abundance. He directed the disciples to tell the people to sit down on the green grass in groups of hundreds and of fifties. Order was established. Then Jesus took the five loaves and the two fish, looked up to heaven, blessed and broke the loaves, and gave them to the disciples to give to the people. Then the fish were likewise divided among the people. Loaf after loaf, fish after fish, the food was distributed so that the five thousand men, plus the women and children, ate their fill and were all satisfied.

Lest there be waste of precious food, the disciples gathered up the broken pieces left over. They filled twelve baskets with the scraps. As earlier Jesus had turned water into wine, on this occasion, he changed scarcity into abundance. On the previous occasion, only a few people knew what Jesus had done while the wedding guests simply rejoiced and drank their fill. On this occasion, the disciples and some in the crowd knew what Jesus had done; but most of the people were simply delighted to have enough to eat. (Perhaps they thought that Zechariah's Catering Company had arrived.) It didn't matter to them how the food came, only that it had come.

But for those who watched this banquet unfold, who had eyes to see what really happened, here was yet another sign. As God had provided manna to sustain the Israelites for forty years in the wilderness, Jesus provided sustenance for the people in that deserted place on that day.

He who was born in Bethlehem (which means house of bread), who was challenged by Satan to turn stones into bread, and who would later describe himself as "the Bread of Life" (John 6:35), was more than able to feed the crowd with both knowledge and food.

For thought or discussion:

- Have you ever, out of curiosity, joined a crowd going to hear a famous speaker or personality?
- Has there ever been a time when your resources expanded far beyond your expectations?
- Do you think that Jesus ever grew weary of the demands that people made on him?

60. Sight to the Blind
Healing the Man Born Blind
John 9

There is sight, and then there is insight. There are people who are physically unable to see, and there are far more people who fail to see and comprehend that which is right before their eyes.

He was born blind, so he had never seen physically. Lacking the sense of sight, he had developed his other senses, especially his sense of hearing and his sense of touch. Even so, in his time, he was relegated to begging. Imagine the things he heard as he sat beside the street, for people often seem to think that a person who can't see is also unable to hear.

The disciples asked Jesus, "Rabbi, who sinned, this man or his parents, that he was born blind?" (9:2). It was likely not the first time that the man had heard people discuss this question, for it was a common belief that physical infirmity was the result of specific sins. Jesus, however, dismissed this notion and said instead that "he was born blind so that God's works might be revealed in him" (9:3). This does not mean that God chose to give the man's parents a blind baby to raise, but rather that God could and would bring unexpected blessing out of even this.

Jesus spat upon the ground, made mud with his saliva, and spread the mud on the man's eyes. Then Jesus told the blind man to go and wash in the pool of Siloam. The man did this, and for the first time, he was able to see. He was given sight by Jesus who had said, in his hearing, "I am the light of the world" (9:5).

The man's neighbors and those who had seen him as a beggar were confused. Was this the man who had been blind or someone who just looked like him? He repeatedly said that he was the man who had been blind. The people asked him how he had come to see, and he told them what Jesus had done for him.

The people brought the man to the Pharisees. They too asked how the man had been given sight, and he testified to them about Jesus. Some of the Pharisees were of the opinion that Jesus could not be a godly man since he had performed this miracle on the sabbath. Other Pharisees argued that a sinful man could not have performed such a sign. They asked the formerly blind man what he had to say about Jesus, and he replied, "He is a prophet" (9:17).

The Jewish leaders did not believe that the man had ever been blind, so they summoned the man's parents. "Is this your son, who you say was born blind? How then does he now see?" (9:19). The parents assured the leaders that this was their son, and that he had been blind from birth. As to how it was that he could now see, that they did not know.

The man who had been blind was again called to appear before the Jewish leaders. They said to him, "Give glory to God! We know that this man [Jesus] is a sinner" (9:24). The healed man responded with a marvelous statement of faith. "I do not know whether he is a sinner. One thing I do know, that though I was blind, now I see" (9:25). The leaders kept arguing with the man and declaring that Jesus could not possibly be from God. To this, the man said, "We know that God does not listen to sinners, but he does listen to one who worships him and obeys his will. Never since the world began has it been heard that anyone opened the eyes of a person born blind. If this man were not from God, he could do nothing" (9:31-33). At that, the leaders reviled him and drove him out.

Jesus found the man and asked him if he believed in the Son of Man. The man said that if he knew who that was, he would believe. Jesus said, "You have seen him, and the one speaking with you is he" (9:37). The man had indeed seen, so he believed and worshiped Jesus.

"Jesus said, 'I came into this world for judgment so that those who do not see may see, and those who do see may become blind'" (9:39). There is sight, and then there is insight. The blind man happily received both.

For thought or discussion:

- Which of your five senses are sharpest and which are less so now?
- What do you think it would be like to have never seen and then to be given the gift of sight?
- When have you seen something but have not really understood what you were seeing?

61. Persistent Faith, Expansive Grace
The Faith of a Foreign Woman
Matthew 15

(Mark 7)

She was another of those unnamed people in the Bible who has much to teach us today.

She was a Gentile (not Jewish) who lived in the region of Tyre and Sidon, north of Galilee. How it is that she knew about Jesus is unclear, but national borders do not necessarily stop the flow of news and information. She had a need, and she believed that Jesus could meet that need.

The woman had a daughter who was demon-possessed. She came to Jesus and "started shouting, 'Have mercy on me, Lord, Son of David; my daughter is tormented by a demon'" (15:22). What was Jesus' initial response? Silence. The only sound she heard was the sound of the disciples urging Jesus, "Send her away, for she keeps shouting after us" (15:23).

To be met by silence in the face of great need is almost unbearable, and yet it is often the experience of those who suffer. She had addressed Jesus with words that indicated both respect and a knowledge of Israel's history and hope. She addressed Jesus as Lord and Son of David. Surely this would result in a positive response. Yet what she first received was silence from Jesus. Was this because he had no compassion? Was this because she was a foreigner and a woman besides? Was Jesus testing her to see if she was truly earnest in her request? As they say, "The Lord only knows." What we do know is that when we are in distress, time seems to stand still, sometimes for far too long.

When Jesus did speak, he said, "I was sent only to the lost sheep of the house of Israel" (15:24.) A less determined person than this woman might have walked off in a huff, but she was not about to let things go so easily. No longer shouting to get Jesus' attention, she came and knelt before him and repeated her request for aid for her daughter. Strident demands were replaced by humble pleas.

The woman's volume ratcheted down, and the depth of her pain was made evident in the simple cry, "Lord, help me" (15:25). Jesus responded with what seems like both a put down and a refusal. He said, "It is not fair to take the children's food and throw it to the dogs" (15:26). These words could have been spoken brusquely and callously, but it is more likely that they were spoken in a tone and with a look on the face and in the eyes that invited and expected a further response.

That is exactly what ensued, for the woman was undeterred by any possible insult or test. Her mission was too important to allow anything to distract her. She said, "Yes, Lord, yet even the dogs eat the crumbs that fall from their master's table." (15:27) Crumbs would be enough if they would bring health to her daughter. So it was. "Jesus answered her, 'Woman, great is your faith! Let it be done for you as you wish.' And her daughter was healed instantly" (15:28).

How easily she could have walked away, but she was convinced that Jesus had the power to drive the demon from her daughter. Neither silence, nor rejection, nor a less than complementary description could stand in her way. By her persistence, she discovered the compassion of Jesus that, though veiled at first, was there all the time. He indeed had the very power she so desperately needed.

For thought or discussion:

- When were you, in the face of the hardship or suffering of another person, moved to seek help?
- Have you ever felt that your pleas for healing or renewal were met by silence?
- When have you had the joy of seeing health and wholeness restored for yourself or for someone you love?

62. I Am
Jesus' Self-Revelation
John

(Matthew 16, Mark 8, Luke 9)

Caesarea Philippi was a city on the lower southwestern slope of Mount Hermon beside the headwaters of the Jordan River. It was the site of temples and shrines dedicated to a variety of deities, including the pagan gods who were worshipped in the time of Jesus.

On one occasion when Jesus and his disciples were in the area, he asked them who people were saying that he was. The disciples said that John the Baptist, Elijah, Jeremiah, or other prophets of old were names that people were using for Jesus. He asked them the all-important question, "But who do you say that I am?" (Matthew 16:15).

Peter spoke up, saying, "You are the Messiah, the Son of the living God" (Matthew 16:16). Jesus affirmed his answer. "Blessed are you, Simon son of Jonah! For flesh and blood has not revealed this to you, but my Father in heaven" (Matthew 16:17).

Peter gave the correct answer, but neither he nor his fellow disciples understood the fullness of that confession. What exactly did it mean for Jesus to be the Messiah — the Christ?

In the Gospel of John, Jesus revealed himself time after time with important descriptors. Speaking with the woman at the well (chapter 4), he described himself as the giver of living water and told her that he was the Messiah. Elsewhere he called himself the Bread of Life (chapter 6), the light of the world (chapters 8 and 9), one who existed before the patriarch Abraham (chapter 8), the gate for the sheep and the Good Shepherd (chapter 10), the resurrection and the life (chapter 11), the way, and the truth, and the life (chapter 14), and the true vine (chapter 15).

Each of these self-revelatory descriptions was spoken by Jesus in a setting where it exactly fit the context. When crowds were looking for Jesus to provide bread, he said that he was the Bread of Life. Regarding the unbelief of the authorities and speaking with the man born blind, Jesus said that he was the light of the world. When it was said that Abraham had greater authority than Jesus, Jesus asserted that he pre-dated Abraham. In explaining his care for his followers, he spoke of being the gate of the sheepfold and also the Good Shepherd. When his dear friend Lazarus died (a story soon to be told), he described himself as the resurrection and the life. When his disciples wondered about the way ahead, Jesus assured them that he was the way, truth, and life. As Jesus celebrated Passover with his disciples, he described himself as the true vine.

Each description was relevant for its situation, but what was most significant is that each image was preceded by the Greek words, *ego eimi,* (which means I am). When the woman at the well said that the Messiah would come, Jesus' response is translated, "I am he," but what he really said was simply "I am." When soldiers and temple police went to arrest Jesus in the garden of Gethsemane (another story yet to be told), he asked them for whom they were looking. They answered, "Jesus of Nazareth." His reply, translated "I am he," was actually pointedly "I am."

What was so important about those statements of Jesus? With each statement, the words of God spoken to Moses on Mount Horeb echoed down the corridors of time and fell on the ears of those to whom Jesus spoke. When Moses asked God for his name, God replied, "I AM WHO I AM." He said further, "Thus you shall say to the Israelites, '*I AM* has sent me to you'" (Exodus 3:14).

The pieces of the puzzle begin to fall into place, and the picture becomes ever clearer. Gabriel announced to Mary that her son would be "called the Son of the Most High" (Luke 1). Of the child Mary would bear, the angel told Joseph, "'and they shall name him Emmanuel,' which means 'God is with us'" (Matthew 1). At Jesus' baptism, the voice from heaven declared, "You are my Son, the Beloved; with you I am well pleased" (Mark 1). Nicodemus was told, "For God so loved the world that he gave his only Son" (John 3). And the Gospel of John begins this way:

In the beginning was the Word, and the Word was with God, and the Word was God. He was in the beginning with God. All things came into being through him, and without him not one thing came into being. What has come into being in him was life, and the life was the light of all people. The light shines in the darkness, and the darkness did not overcome it…And the Word became flesh and lived among us…full of grace and truth (1:1-5, 14).

For thought or discussion:

- Which of the descriptions of Jesus speaks most profoundly to you?
- How do all these descriptions of Jesus help you to understand who he is?
- From your life and faith experiences, are there descriptive phrases you would add?

63. Mountains High and Valleys Low

Transfiguration and Exorcism
Matthew 17, Mark 9, Luke 9

Taking a hike up a mountain can be exhilarating and surprising. The obvious assumption is that there will be spectacular views along the way, especially from the top of the mountain. Surprises can happen at any point along the path.

On one occasion, Jesus took Peter, James, and John on such a hike, and what happened at the top was surprising indeed. Jesus may not have been surprised, but the three disciples definitely were.

Jesus was transfigured so that his face shone like the sun and his clothes became dazzling white. As it had been with Moses when he met with God on Mount Sinai (Exodus 34), so it was with Jesus. That was surprising enough, but there was more. Suddenly Moses and Elijah appeared, talking with Jesus. Here were the prime representatives of the law and of the prophets. "They appeared in glory and were speaking of [Jesus'] departure, which he was about to accomplish at Jerusalem" (Luke 9:31).

Dumbfounded and terrified, Peter blurted out, "Rabbi, it is good for us to be here; let us make three dwellings, one for you, one for Moses, and one for Elijah" (Mark 9:5). None of the disciples really knew what to say, but it seemed that it might be a good idea to at least show hospitality to these two men of old, and perhaps to make the moment somewhat permanent.

Adding glory to glory, a bright cloud descended, and from the cloud came a voice saying, "This is my Son, the beloved; with him I am well pleased; listen to him!" (Matthew 17:5). Yet more terrified, the disciples fell to the ground. But Jesus touched them and told them not to be afraid. "And when they looked up, they saw no one except Jesus himself alone" (Matthew 17:8).

As the men descended the mountain, Jesus told the three disciples to tell no one what they had seen "until after the Son of Man has been raised from the dead" (Matthew 17:9). This must have confounded them even more, for they were still trying to process what they had just experienced. How could they make any sense of this talk of being raised from the dead?

It seems that what are called mountaintop experiences, times of great inspiration and transformation, are almost always followed by a strong dose of reality. The top of the mountain is exchanged for the depth of the valley. Times of retreat are replaced by the shock of reentry.

When Jesus, Peter, James, and John came to the other disciples, they encountered a crowd of people and a clearly unsettled situation. Here were people who were not contemplating a heavenly vision, but who were trying to make sense of the illnesses and brokenness that were so pervasive in life.

A man in the crowd ran up to Jesus and begged him to heal his son. The man told Jesus that his son had a spirit that had possessed him since childhood and that it had frequently seized him and thrown him to the ground or into the fire or into the water. The disciples had been unable to cure the boy. He continued, "but if you are able to do anything, have pity on us and help us" (Mark 9:22). Jesus said that everything is possible for the one who believes. "Immediately the father of the child cried out, 'I believe; help my unbelief!'" (Mark 9:24). Jesus cast out the unclean spirit and restored the boy to full health.

The disciples asked Jesus why they had been unable to heal the boy. He used this as a teaching opportunity to talk to them about the power and importance of both prayer and faith. Just like all of us, the disciples still had so much to learn from Jesus.

For thought or discussion:

- How do you think that Peter, James, and John knew that the two men were Moses and Elijah?
- Have you ever had what you would regard as a mountaintop experience?
- Did that experience have only a temporary impact, or has it continued throughout your life?
- How would you have felt if you were one of the nine disciples who did not accompany Jesus to the Mount of Transfiguration?

(In church tradition and on liturgical calendars, the Tranfiguration is celebrated at a variety of times, usually in August. In the Lutheran tradition, the Tranfiguration is celebrated on the final Sunday of the Epiphany Season, occurring, depending on the date of Easter, between the first Sunday in February and the first Sunday in March. The liturgical color is white.)

64. To See With Jesus' Eyes

The Question of Greatness
Matthew 18 & 20

(Mark 9 & 10, Luke 9, 18, 22)

Jesus had a way of turning things upside down. His teachings and his actions were often the opposite of what would have been expected or deemed proper, especially by the religious leaders of his time.

The disciples asked him who is the greatest in the kingdom of heaven? You would expect that his answer would have focused on saints or martyrs who had given their lives for the faith. Or perhaps he would laud some notable Jewish leaders. Maybe the disciples themselves would be singled out for praise.

Instead, he set a child in their midst and said, "Truly I tell you, unless you change and become like children, you will never enter the kingdom of heaven" (18:3). He then went on to say how much these little ones were valued and how important it was to do nothing to lead them astray or neglect them.

Not long after that, little children were being brought to Jesus to receive his blessing. The disciples sought to prevent this interruption in Jesus' schedule, but Jesus would have none of it. He said, "Let the little children come to me, and do not stop them; for it is to such as these that the kingdom of heaven belongs" (19:14).

In that time, children were seen as having little value, but Jesus elevated them as perfect models of the kingdom. It is not that we are to remain limited in mentality or ability as children are. It is that we are to have the innocence and trust that characterize children. We are to be aware of our own neediness and to seek the protection and nurture of God. We are to delight in emulating our Heavenly Father.

Not long after these events, James and John (or perhaps their mother on their behalf) came to Jesus with a request that they be allowed to sit, one at his right hand and one at his left hand in his kingdom. The desire for places of honor consumed them, perhaps enhanced by Jesus choosing them (along with Peter) to witness the Transfiguration. Clearly, they had not listened carefully to his teaching regarding the children.

When the other ten disciples heard this, they were angry. Likely as not they each had designs on favored treatment for themselves and didn't appreciated this bold-faced power grab by James and John.

Jesus had more teaching to do. First, he told the brothers that the specific places of honor would be decided by his Father. Then he addressed the twelve: "You know that the rulers of the Gentiles lord it over them, and their great ones are tyrants over them. It will not be so among you; but whoever wishes to be great among you must be your servant, and whoever wishes to be first among you must be your slave; just as the Son of Man came not be be served but to serve, and to give his life a ransom for many" (20:25-28).

Time after time, by his teachings and by his actions, Jesus sought to make it clear to those who would follow him that God does not see as the world sees. What the world tends to value, things like wealth, power, and possessions, is not what God values. God desires humility, kindness, love, compassion, forgiveness, faithfulness, and obedience. These are the signs of true greatness in the kingdom. (Remember the Beatitudes in the Sermon on the Mount?) Those who seek these things are regarded as great in the kingdom of heaven, for such people are learning to see as Jesus sees and to do as Jesus does.

For thought or discussion:

- Of all the people you know, who do you most regard as a truly great person?
- What qualities do you look for and value in other people?
- What does it mean for you to have a childlike (not a childish) faith?

65. The Namesake of the 'Good Sam Club'

The Good Samaritan
Luke 10

Jesus often taught by using parables. These were stories that made use of common images or experiences to make a point. Parables were easy to remember. Parables seemed simple, but often, as the hearers reflected on the story, the point to be made was extremely challenging. Parables have been called "earthly stories with heavenly meanings."

One such parable is known as "The Good Samaritan." Here was an oxymoron, for as we saw when Jesus met with the woman at the well in John, chapter four, Samaritans were seen by the Jews as impure and untrustworthy — people to be avoided.

Jesus told this parable in response to a lawyer's question regarding what he needed to do to inherit eternal life. Jesus asked him what was written in the law, and he rightly answered, "You shall love the Lord your God with all your heart, and with all your soul, and with all your strength, and with all your mind; and your neighbor as yourself" (10:27). Jesus affirmed this answer and told the man to do this. "But wanting to justify himself, he asked Jesus, 'And who is my neighbor?'" (10:29).

Jesus told about a man who was traveling the road from Jerusalem to Jericho when he was beset by robbers who stripped him, beat him, and left him lying beside the road, half dead. People would have understood this image, for that road was notoriously dangerous. In about twenty miles, that narrow, rocky, and winding road descended over three thousand feet, and it was a perfect setting for robbers to ply their trade. Traveling this road alone made one an easy mark.

A priest, who was traveling on the same road, saw the man and passed by on the other side of the road. And then a Levite came along and did the same. Once again, the hearers of the parable would have nodded in understanding. While they might well have empathized with the poor man beside the road, they would have seen the wisdom of those two Jewish religious leaders. For one thing, in the event that the man was truly dead, touching him would have made the two men ceremonially unclean, and that would have prevented them from doing their duties in the temple. For another thing, it was often the ploy of robbers to have one man lie beside the road as a victim. Then, when travelers stopped to give aid, the other robbers would attack them all. Best to hurry on as quickly as possible before becoming a victim yourself.

The third traveler was a Samaritan. The hearers might have jumped to the conclusion that the Samaritan was, in fact, the robber or at least a friend of such people. In fact, this man was compassionate and caring. Without hesitation he came to the aid of the man beside the road. He bound up his wounds, placed him on his animal, took him to an inn, and cared for him there. The next day, he paid the innkeeper and then instructed him, "Take care of him; and when I come back, I will repay you whatever more you spend" (10:35). Whatever else this Samaritan traveler may have been, he was known to the innkeeper to be an honest and generous man; and he showed himself to be a person of deep compassion.

Jesus then asked the lawyer, "'Which of these three, do you think, was a neighbor to the man who fell into the hands of the robbers?' He said, 'The one who showed him mercy.' Jesus said to him, 'Go and do likewise'" (10:36-37).

The lawyer had asked a question that would allow him to determine how small a circle he could draw and still fulfill the commandment to love his neighbor. Was it enough to love his immediate physical neighbors? Did the circle need to expand to include all those of his own race? Who could he ignore without violating God's command?

Jesus, however, answered the question by turning it on its head. It was no longer, "Who is my neighbor?" Now it was, "What does it mean to act as a neighbor?" The call of God is not to draw circles of inclusion but to show mercy to all who are in need. The final sentence rings out loudly and clearly, "Go and do likewise."

For thought or discussion:

- Has there been a time when you, in concern or pity for someone else, helped a stranger?
- Have you passed by a person who was calling out for assistance? When and why?
- Have you benefited from a stranger stopping to assist you in a time of trial or need?

66. Discovering Life

Mary, Martha, and Lazarus
John 11

The closer the friendship, the more helpful one wants to be, especially in times of need.

Jesus was close to Lazarus and his sisters, Mary and Martha, who lived in the village of Bethany, a couple miles east of Jerusalem. So it was that when Lazarus became deathly ill, the sisters sent word to Jesus. They knew that he loved them, and they were sure that he would hurry to them and heal their brother.

Strange as it seems, Jesus' response to this news was to say to his disciples, "This illness does not lead to death; rather it is for God's glory, so that the Son of God may be glorified through it" (11:4). Having said this, he stayed where he was for two days before leaving for Bethany. Lazarus died.

It was true that the Jewish religious leaders in Judea had sought to stone Jesus, so the thought of returning to that area might have seemed reckless. When someone we love is in dire need, however, we are willing to take risks to assist. It was not fear that delayed Jesus. It was a higher purpose.

Jesus said to his disciples, "Our friend Lazarus has fallen asleep, but I am going there to awaken him" (11:11). This struck the disciples as odd, for they reasoned that if Lazarus was simply sleeping, he would not need Jesus' intervention. Jesus told them plainly that Lazarus was dead.

By the time Jesus and his disciples came near Bethany, Lazarus had been in the tomb for four days. When Martha heard that Jesus was near, she went to meet him. She spoke a word that was both chastisement and hope. "Lord, if you had been here, my brother would not have died. But even now I know that God will give you whatever you ask of him" (11:21-22). Jesus said that Lazarus would rise again; Martha affirmed that he would rise in the resurrection on the last day. "Jesus said to her, 'I am the resurrection and the life. Those who believe in me, even though they die, will live, and everyone who lives and believes in me will never die. Do you believe this?' She said to him, 'Yes,

Lord, I believe that you are the Messiah, the Son of God, the one coming into the world'" (11:25-27).

Martha went back to the house to get her sister. When Mary came to Jesus, she knelt before him, weeping. Echoing her sister's word of disappointment, she said, "Lord, if you had been here, my brother would not have died" (11:32).

Jesus, deeply moved by the grief of the sisters and of the people who had come to console them, wept. The people were moved by Jesus' evident love for Lazarus, but some wondered, "Could not he who opened the eyes of the blind man have kept this man from dying?" (11:37).

Jesus, Mary and Martha, the disciples, and the mourners went to the tomb. It was a cave with a stone rolled across the opening.

At Jesus' request that the stone be removed, Martha said there would be a stench since Lazarus had been dead for four days. "Jesus said to her, 'Did I not tell you that if you believed, you would see the glory of God?'" (11:40). The stone was removed.

Jesus, looking heavenward, spoke to God, and then he cried with a loud voice, "Lazarus, come out!" (11:43). And out he came! He was all bound up with strips of cloth, and his face was wrapped in a cloth. Jesus said, "Unbind him, and let him go" (11:44). And so they did. Lazarus was alive again, and there was great rejoicing.

Not everyone rejoiced. When the religious leaders in Jerusalem learned of this miracle, they were greatly concerned. "If we let him go on like this, everyone will believe in him, and the Romans will come and destroy both our holy place and our nation" (11:48.) But Caiaphas, the high priest, said, "You do not understand that it is better for you to have one man die for the people than to have the whole nation destroyed" (11:50). From that day, they looked for a way to put Jesus to death.

Lazarus had become a celebrity of sorts (since it is not every day that a person is restored to life), and since the raising of Lazarus added to Jesus' fame, the chief priests also planned to kill Lazarus. Evil has a way of fostering more evil, and fear generates more fear.

For thought or discussion:

- Have you kept the vigil beside the bed of a dying family member and prayed for life?
- Is it okay to be upset with God as Mary and Martha were upset with Jesus for coming too late?
- What do you think that Lazarus thought when Jesus called him back to life?

67. Lost and Found

The Prodigal Son
Luke 15

"Now all the tax collectors and sinners were coming near to listen to [Jesus]. And the Pharisees and the scribes were grumbling and saying, 'This fellow welcomes sinners and eats with them'" (15:1-2). In response, Jesus told them three parables.

He told of a shepherd who lost one of his hundred sheep and, leaving the ninety-nine, searched for the lost sheep until he had found it and returned it to the flock. He told of a woman who lost a precious silver coin and swept her house until she had found it. In each case, friends and neighbors were invited to come and celebrate and share in the joy of restoration. Just so, Jesus said, there is great rejoicing in heaven over one sinner who repents.

Then he told a third parable about a man and his two sons.

One day the younger son came to his father and asked to receive his inheritance. While we may read that request with sympathy for the boy who wanted to get on with his life and make his way in the world, in Jesus' day, what the boy essentially said to his father was, *Why don't you drop dead so that I can have my money?* Imagine what sort of response that would likely have elicited from his father.

In this case, amazingly, the father granted his son's request. Doing so required him to liquidate assets (not likely at the most favorable price) and to diminish his own estate.

With wealth in hand, the younger son traveled to a distant country and had the time of his life. Living the high life, however, is costly; and it was not long before he had squandered all of his inheritance. Easy come, easy go. Having wasted his money in riotous living, he became destitute; and at the same time, a severe famine occurred in the country where he lived. The only job he could find was tending pigs, not exactly desirable work for a kosher lad. He was at the bottom of the heap.

Sitting among the swine, he came to his senses. "How many of my father's hired hands have bread enough and to spare, but here I am dying of hunger!" (15:17).

He decided that, hat in hand, he would go back to his father and plead for mercy. As he went, he rehearsed his speech. "Father, I have sinned against heaven and before you; I am no longer worthy to be called your son; treat me like one of your hired hands" (15:18-19). He had every reason to expect a frosty reception from his father and the scorn of his hometown folk.

But his father, catching sight of him while he was still a good way from home, hitched up his robes and ran to his son. He kissed him and embraced him. Obviously, the father had been waiting, hoping, and watching for his dearly loved son to return. As the young man began his crow-eating speech, his father cut him off mid-sentence. He told the servants to fetch the best robe, sandals, and a ring; to kill the fatted calf, and to make ready a feast, "for this son of mine was dead and is alive again; he was lost and is found!" (15:24). The homecoming party began.

There was also an older son who had stayed at home to tend the family businesses. When the younger son returned, his brother was in the fields. As he drew near to the house, he heard the sounds of merrymaking. He asked one of the servants what was going on, and he was told of his brother's return. This enraged him, and he refused to go into the house and to join the party.

The father went out to his older son and entreated him to come to the party. "But he answered his father, 'Listen! For all these years I have been working like a slave for you, and I have never disobeyed your command; yet you have never given me even a young goat so that I might celebrate with my friends. But when this son of yours came back, who has devoured your property with prostitutes, you killed the fatted calf for him!'" (15:29-30). He was clearly incensed by his father's open-armed welcome of the brother he resented, and he had no interest in letting bygones be bygones. After all, his brother, having blown his inheritance, would now be consuming more of the family's estate, further diminishing what would ultimately come to the first-born son. By contrast, his own steadfastness should have been duly lauded and rewarded.

Whereas the older son was angry and only referred to the prodigal son as "this son of yours," the father said, "Son, you are always with me, and all that is mine is yours. But we had to celebrate and rejoice, because this brother of yours was dead and has come to life; he was lost and has been found" (15:31-32).

Scandals abound in this parable. The younger son's request and the father's acquiescence would have set heads shaking. The fact that the father hiked up his robes, exposed his legs, and ran down the road was unseemly at best, since elders properly walked in stately fashion. Freely welcoming back his son instead of making him crawl and grovel to earn again, little by little, a place in the household would have caused tongues to wag. The older son's refusal to come to the party would have been an equal affront to the father, for it was the older son's responsibility to oversee the party and to meet the needs of the guests. All this and the pigsty too.

What God desires, however, is that all of the children should be safely and happily at home.

For thought or discussion:

- With whom in this parable do you most easily identify?
- Can you see yourself in some measure in each of the characters (hopefully not the fatted calf)?
- Are you ever scandalized by God's love, grace, forgiveness, and mercy?

68. To Leap, Perchance to Kneel

Healing the Lepers
Luke 17

To be a leper in Jesus' time was truly to be an outcast.

The instructions for dealing with lepers are found in Leviticus, chapters thirteen and fourteen. It was the responsibility of the priests to examine people with suspected cases of leprosy. "The person who has the leprous disease shall wear torn clothes and let the hair of his head be disheveled; and he shall cover his upper lip and cry out, 'Unclean, unclean.' He shall remain unclean as long as he has the disease; he is unclean. He shall live alone; his dwelling shall be outside the camp" (Leviticus 13:45-46). For Jewish people, this meant that a leper was both physically and ceremonially to be avoided. To be a leper was to be cut off from home and family and, if the disease was chronic, to almost certainly live in poverty. It was only the priest who could, after determining that the person was cured, restore him or her to the community of the healthy and the clean.

Jesus was on his way to Jerusalem, traveling through the region between Galilee and Samaria, when he was met by ten lepers. They kept their distance, but they called to Jesus, "Jesus, Master, have mercy on us!" (17:13). Jesus' response was very simple. He told the ten lepers to go and show themselves to the priests. As they went on their way, they realized that they had been cured, restored, renewed, set free.

What would your response have been, do you suppose, if you had been one of those ten? Would you have leapt for joy, danced around, and rejoiced? Would there have been anything hindering you from making a beeline to the nearest priest?

Such was the response of those lepers. Home and family would once again be theirs. Being shunned would be replaced by being embraced. Tears of joy would surely flow, and a party would ensue. All that they needed to do was to find a priest and be declared clean.

One of the lepers, however, realizing that he was healed, had something else on his mind. He turned around, and praising God with a loud voice, he went back to Jesus. He fell on his knees at Jesus' feet and thanked him. This man was a Samaritan.

"Then Jesus asked, 'Were not ten made clean? But the other nine, where are they? Was none of them found to return and give praise to God except this foreigner?' Then he said to [the Samaritan], 'Get up and go on your way; your faith has made you well'" (17:17-19).

All ten lepers were healed. All ten were filled with overwhelming relief and gratitude. All ten leaped for joy. But only one remembered to give thanks to the giver of the gift.

For thought or discussion:

- Have you ever received a gift for which you failed to thank the giver?
- Have you given a gift to someone who delighted to receive it but failed to say, "thank you"?
- Does giving thanks to the giver of a gift enhance your appreciation of it?

69. Go Climb a Tree

Zaccheus
Luke 19

Zaccheus was rich, and he was hated. He was a tax collector, and under the best of circumstances, people tend to be less than pleased with paying taxes. In Israel in Jesus' day, the paying of taxes was especially odious, for the taxes were paid to the oppressive government of Rome. Jewish people who worked for the Romans to collect these taxes were therefore despised. Since Zaccheus was the chief tax collector for Jericho, he was especially hated. He was indeed rich, and for the record, he was short in stature.

As Jesus and his disciples made their way to Jerusalem, they passed through Jericho.

As is normal when a famous person comes to town, crowds of people gathered around Jesus. They had heard of him, and many had listened to him speak and seen him perform miracles. They came to see him, perhaps to touch him, and maybe even to be healed by him. Surely, he would have something to tell them that would encourage them. And they walked along, jostling one another, trying to get close to Jesus.

Zaccheus was also intrigued and wanted to see Jesus; but since the crowd was dense and he was short, he could not catch more than a glimpse of Jesus. Not to be deterred, he ran ahead and climbed a sycamore tree that grew beside the road on which Jesus was walking. This was not the sort of thing one would expect of a wealthy tax collector. Yet there he was, perched on a limb of the tree.

When Jesus came to the tree, he looked up and saw Zaccheus. No doubt the townsfolk were amused at the sight, and likely they expected that Jesus would heap scorn on Zaccheus. Here was a perfect opportunity for Jesus to say all the things that they themselves thought about this hated tax collector. Jesus would surely denounce him as a disgrace to his people, as a parasite, as a traitor, and as a despicable human being. Shame would cover him like a cloak. Jesus might even make a snarky comment about how all the wealth he had amassed could not prevent Zacchaeus from being a little man.

"When Jesus came to the place, he looked up and said to him, 'Zacchaeus, hurry and come down; for I must stay at your house today'" (19:5).

Had the people heard correctly? How could it be that Jesus would pass up an opportunity to denounce and instead choose to dine with Zacchaeus? They grumbled and said, "He has gone to be the guest of one who is a sinner" (19:7). How very like Jesus to do this.

Zacchaeus was a changed man. He said to Jesus, "Look, half of my possessions, Lord, I will give to the poor; and if I have defrauded anyone of anything, I will pay back four times as much" (19:8). It may well have been that Zacchaeus was, all along, a basically honest man. If he had gained all his wealth by fraud, his words to Jesus were hollow, for he would not have been able to repay each person four times over, having first given half of his possessions to the poor. Had he been wrongly painted with the broad brush of hatred and distrust of tax collectors?

"Then Jesus said to him, 'Today salvation has come to this house, because he too is a son of Abraham. For the Son of Man came to seek out and to save the lost'" (19:9-10).

This is the perfect segue to the story next to be told.

For thought or discussion:

- Do you ever judge people because of their professions without really getting to know them?
- Have you ever put yourself in an embarrassing position to see someone important?
- Have you had a life-changing experience that radically changed your view of your possessions?

70. The King Has Come

Palm Sunday
Matthew 21:1-21, Mark 11:1-11, Luke 19:28-44, John 12:12-19

It began with a parade of sorts. There was a single unit, a man riding on a donkey.

The preparations for the parade had been quite simple. As Jesus and his disciples were approaching Jerusalem, he sent two of his disciples to the village of Bethphage, near the Mount of Olives, to fetch a young donkey on which no one had ever ridden. If an objection was raised to their taking the colt, they were to say, "The Lord needs it and will send it back here immediately" (Mark 11:3). The disciples brought the donkey to Jesus, spread their cloaks on it, and Jesus sat on it. The parade was underway.

There are two wonders here. The first is that the owners of the colt so readily complied with the disciples' taking of the animal. Whether or not this had been prearranged, we do not know, but in any case, compliance was immediate. The second wonder is that Jesus sat on the colt and it made no effort to throw him. Here was an animal that had never been ridden, and yet it willingly allowed Jesus to ride. There was harmony between Jesus and the donkey.

Jerusalem was filled with its own residents, as well as the multitude of pilgrims who had come to the city to celebrate Passover. This particular year, there was a buzz regarding Jesus of Nazareth. Could he possibly be the Messiah for whom Israel had so long waited? If he was in fact the promised Messiah, would he drive out the hated Romans and take the throne of David? Was a new and glorious era about to begin?

As Jesus drew near the city, a crowd welcomed him, throwing their cloaks on the road ahead of him and waving branches of palms and other trees. They shouted, "Hosanna! Blessed is the one who comes in the name of the Lord! Blessed is the coming kingdom of our ancestor David! Hosanna in the highest heaven!" (Mark 11:9-10). When some Pharisees in the crowd told Jesus to command the people to stop their chants of praise, Jesus said, "I tell you, if these were silent, the stones would shout out" (Luke 19:40).

It was customary for a king or a conquerer to majestically enter a city riding on a mighty war horse or in a chariot. Jesus, however, came humbly. Matthew reminds us (Matthew 21:4-5) that this fulfilled the words of the Old Testament prophet, Zechariah, "Rejoice greatly, O daughter Zion! Shout aloud, O daughter Jerusalem! Lo, your king comes to you; triumphant and victorious is he, humble and riding on a donkey, on a colt, the foal of a donkey" (Zechariah 9:9).

The promised Son of David had arrived, and the people were filled with expectancy. The true and righteous King had come and would indeed, ascend his throne. Yet Jesus was not the sort of king the crowds expected, and the throne that he would ascend was far different than they could have imagined. The events of the days ahead would make that abundantly clear.

For thought or discussion:

- What do you think were the hopes of the people who greeted Jesus when he came to Jerusalem?
- How would your hopes be similar or different if Jesus came to you today?
- What traits do you most admire in people who are in positions of leadership?

(In church tradition and on liturgical calendars, Palm or Passion Sunday is the beginning of holy week, and it is celebrated on the Sunday before Easter. The liturgical color for Palm Sunday is purple. The liturgical color for Passion Sunday is scarlet.)

71. The Week That Was

Holy Week
Matthew 21:12–26:16, Mark 11:12–14:11, Luke 19:45–22:6, John 12:20-56

Before continuing with the story, it is important to note how crucial the events of this week were to the writers of the four gospels. Mark's telling of the gospel, for example, is sixteen chapters in length. His narrative begins with the baptism of Jesus and so covers basically three years. Almost the entirety of those three years of Jesus' public ministry are covered in ten chapters. The remaining six chapters (37.5% of the gospel) are devoted to this single week, and the final three chapters deal with three days. Clearly, for Mark, this truly is the week that was. The other three gospel writers likewise see these events as the climax of the story and as that for which the rest of the accounts are recorded.

What transpired in those days? The writers have slightly different emphases, and the details vary somewhat, but essentially these are the things that happened: the cleansing of the temple, the anointing in Bethany, the plot to betray Jesus, the preparations for the Passover, Jesus' meal with his disciples, the prayer in the garden of Gethsemane, the arrest and trial, the mistreatment at the hands of the Roman soldiers, the crucifixion, and the burial. Each day, Jesus taught in the temple; and each evening, Jesus and his disciples went to Bethany and spent the night there. Throughout the week, the hostility of the Jewish leaders toward Jesus intensified, and in the end, Jesus was executed by the Romans.

The next stories will deal with the Passover, arrest, trial, crucifixion, and burial. Here we flesh out the earlier events of the week.

It began with an incident that is shocking to many, for their image of Jesus is that he was always gentle. In fact, the gospels show us a Jesus who was motivated by love and compassion, but who was also passionate about truth, justice, and righteousness. Jesus, entering the temple, overturned the tables of the money changers and the seats of those who sold doves and drove them out of the temple. While the exchanging of money and the selling of birds and animals had originally been set up to make it possible for pilgrims to procure the things they needed to make the appropriate sacrifices, as time went by, the merchants took advantage of the pilgrims to increase their own profits. Jesus said, "Is it not written, 'My house shall be called a house of prayer for all the nations'? But you have made it a den of robbers" (Mark 11:17). Jesus' actions were not likely well received by the merchants or by those who profited from their activities.

This added more fuel to the fire of those religious leaders who were looking for a way to get rid of Jesus. He was a threat to the economic status quo. He was a threat to their entrenched power. He openly denounced them for their hypocrisy. He, like false messiahs who had come before him, was likely going to attract the negative attention of the Roman authorities; and nothing good would come from that. As Caiaphas, the high priest, had declared to the Jewish council after Jesus had raised Lazarus to life, "it is better for you to have one man die for the people than to have the whole nation destroyed" (John 11:50).

The religious leaders tried to verbally entrap Jesus. They asked him what authority he had for the things that he said and did. He responded by saying that he would answer their question if they first answered his question regarding John the Baptist's baptism, whether it was from heaven or of human origin. They were on the horns of a dilemma. If they said it was from heaven, he would ask them why they didn't believe John. If they said it was of human origin, the people would be in an uproar, for they regarded John as a prophet. Since the leaders declined to answer Jesus' question, he declined to answer their question about the source of his authority.

They tried again, asked him about paying taxes to the emperor. If he said to pay the taxes, he would incur the displeasure of the people, and they might cease to follow him. If he said not to pay the taxes, he would be guilty of sedition, and they could report him to the Romans as one fomenting insurrection. Jesus asked to see a coin and then asked the people whose likeness and inscription were on it. They said that the emperor's likeness and inscription were on the coin. Then he said, "Give to the emperor the things that are the emperor's, and to God the things that are God's" (Mark 12:17). Once again, those who sought to trap Jesus failed.

During that week, Jesus spoke with his disciples about things that would come to pass: the destruction of the temple, persecutions that they would endure, the destruction of Jerusalem, the signs of the end of the age, and the coming of the Son of Man. He told them to be faithful and watchful. No doubt, they were confused by what he said.

One night, in Bethany, Jesus was a guest in the home of Simon the leper. During the meal, a woman came with an alabaster jar of very expensive ointment of nard. She poured the ointment on Jesus' head. Some of those in the house were aghast, saying that the ointment could have been sold for a good price, and the money could have been given to the poor. They began to scold the woman. Jesus, however, said, "She has performed a good service for me. For you always have the poor with you, and you can show kindness to them whenever you wish; but you will not always have me. She has...anointed my body beforehand for its burial. Truly I tell you, wherever the good news is proclaimed in the whole world, what she has done will be told in remembrance of her" (Mark 14:6-9).

Judas Iscariot, one of Jesus' twelve disciples, went to the chief priests to offer, for a price, to betray Jesus. They agreed to pay him thirty pieces of silver, and from that moment he began looking for an opportunity. Why did he do this? We cannot know for certain what was in Judas' mind and heart. He may have simply been greedy. He may have become disenchanted with Jesus. Or he may have grown tired of waiting for Jesus to make his move and usher in anew the Davidic kingdom. If the latter was the case, he may have been trying to force Jesus' hand. His motive was unclear; his actions were not.

For thought or discussion:

- How do you understand the conflicts and hostility that are revealed in these stories?
- What do you think belongs to "the emperor," and what do you think belongs to God?
- What do you think was Judas' motive?

72. An Upper Room and a Garden

Maundy Thursday

Matthew 26:17-75, Mark 14:12-72, Luke 22:7-71, John 13:1–18:27

Then came the day for celebrating the Passover. Jesus sent Peter and John to make the preparations for the meal. They asked him where this should be done. "'Listen,' he said to them, 'when you have entered the city, a man carrying a jar of water will meet you; follow him into the house he enters…[the owner of the house] will show you a large room upstairs, already furnished. Make preparations for us there'" (Luke 22:10 and 12),

Jesus and his disciples gathered to share the Passover. The celebration traditionally began with the question, "Why is this night different from all other nights?" This led to the retelling of the story of God's deliverance of the people of Israel from bondage in Egypt. This particular Passover was the genesis of two new and significant things that promised deliverance for all people from bondage in sin.

Jesus girded himself with a towel and began to wash the feet of the disciples. This was the task of the lowest slave, not of the leader of the group or the master of the house. When he came to Peter, "Peter said to him, 'You will never wash my feet.' Jesus answered, 'Unless I wash you, you have no share with me'" (John 13:8). He then told his disciples that they were to emulate him in lives of loving and humble service. "I give you a new commandment, that you love one another. Just as I have loved you, you also should love one another. By this everyone will know that you are my disciples, if you have love for one another" (John 13:34-35). This day of holy week is called Maundy Thursday. *Maundy* is derived from the Latin word for "command."

As Jesus and his disciples sat at table that evening, he told them that one of them would betray him. While Judas knew that this was true, none of the others had any idea that such a heinous thing could possibly occur. They began to ask which one of them it could be. (By the way, this moment of confusion and angst is the subject of Leonardo daVinci's famous fresco of "The Last Supper.") Even when Jesus said, "It is the one to whom I give this piece of bread when I have dipped it in the dish," (John

13:26) and gave the bread to Judas, the disciples were still in a state of shock, confusion, and denial.

Jesus then transformed this Passover meal by taking first bread and then one of the cups of wine and instituted the Lord's Supper. "Now as they were eating, Jesus took bread, and blessed, and broke it, and gave it to the disciples and said, 'Take, eat; this is my body.' And he took a cup, and when he had given thanks he gave it to them, saying, 'Drink of it, all of you; for this is my blood of the covenant, which is poured out for many for the forgiveness of sins'" (Matthew 26:26-28 RSV). Ever after, those who follow Jesus have shared this holy meal in which he is forever present.

When the meal was ended, they all sang a hymn and went out to the Mount of Olives. On the way, Jesus announced that the disciples would forsake him that very night. Peter declared that he would never desert Jesus, but Jesus said that before the rooster crowed, Peter would deny him three times.

On the Mount of Olives, they entered the garden of Gethsemane. Jesus told his disciples to sit there while he went to pray. "He took with him Peter and James and John, and began to be distressed and agitated. He said to them, 'I am deeply grieved, even to death; remain here, and keep awake'" (Mark 14:33-34). Going a little farther, he fell on the ground and prayed in deep agony, saying, "Abba, Father, for you all things are possible; remove this cup from me; yet, not what I want, but what you want" (Mark 14:36). Returning to the three disciples, he found them sleeping. Twice more he went and prayed the same prayers, and twice more he came and found the disciples asleep. Then he told them, "The hour has come; the Son of Man is betrayed into the hands of sinners. Get up, let us be going. See, my betrayer is at hand" (Mark 14:41-42).

Indeed, Judas had come accompanied by a crowd, armed with swords and clubs, who had been sent by the chief priests and elders. Judas had told the people with him that the man he kissed was the man they should arrest. As the crowd approached him, Jesus asked them for whom they were looking. "They answered, 'Jesus of Nazareth.' Jesus replied, 'I am he (*ego eimi*, literally "I am")'" (John 18:5). Coming up to Jesus, Judas kissed him; and the people seized Jesus.

One of the disciples (John tells us that it was Peter) sprang into action. Drawing his sword and swinging wildly, he cut off the right ear of one of the high priest's servants, a man named Malchus. "Then Jesus said to him, 'Put your sword back into its place; for all who take the sword will perish by the sword. Do you think that I cannot appeal to my Father, and he will at once send me more than twelve legions of angels? But how then would the scriptures be fulfilled, which say it must happen in this way?'" (Matthew 26:52-54). Touching Malchus' ear, Jesus healed him.

The disciples deserted Jesus and fled. Mark adds: "A certain young man was following him, wearing nothing but a linen cloth. They caught hold of him, but he left the linen cloth and ran off naked" (Mark 14:51-52). (Why would Mark, whose gospel narrative is the sparest, have included this detail unless he himself was that young man?)

Jesus was taken to the house of Caiaphas where the chief priests, elders and scribes had assembled. Peter followed as far as the courtyard of the house, and there he sat warming himself by the fire. The members of the council were looking for testimony against Jesus so they could put him to death. Many gave false testimony, but no two agreed in the witness they gave. Finally, Caiaphas asked Jesus directly if he was the Messiah, the Son of God. Jesus' response was, "I am; and 'you will see the Son of Man seated at the right hand of the Power,' and 'coming with the clouds of heaven'" (Mark 14:62). At this the high priest tore his robes and said, "Why do we still need witnesses? You have heard his blasphemy! What is your decision?" (Mark 14:63-64). They all agreed that Jesus deserved to die. Some of the people spat at him, blindfolded him, struck him, and said, "Prophesy!"

At that very moment, Jesus' prophecy was being fulfilled. In the courtyard, Peter was asked by a servant girl if he was with Jesus. He denied even knowing Jesus. Later another servant girl asked him the same question, and again he denied it. When he was asked a third time if he knew or was with Jesus, "he began to curse, and he swore an oath, 'I do not know this man you are talking about'" (Mark 14:71). These words were barely out of Peter's mouth when the rooster crowed. Peter remembered Jesus' words, and he went out and wept bitterly.

For thought or discussion:

- What emotions do you think the disciples felt as that momentous evening/night unfolded?
- How is Jesus' command to love one another a key to understanding both the Christian life and the Lord's Supper?
- Have you ever felt that you betrayed or denied Jesus?

(In church tradition and on liturgical calendars, Maundy Thursday is three days before Easter. It is the beginning of the Easter Triduum, the three most holy days. The Maundy Thursday service often includes foot washing plus the stripping and cleaning of the altar. The service always includes Holy Communion.)

73. High and Lifted Up

The Crucifixion
Matthew 27, Mark 15, Luke 23, John 18:28--19:42

When it was morning, the chief priests, scribes, and elders took Jesus to Pontius Pilate, the Roman governor or procurator.

Pilate was the man with the power. He controlled the Roman legions; and he was the emperor's agent, charged with maintaining the peace of Rome in the province of Judea. Though little was historically recorded about Pilate, it was thought that he was an able, strong, and sometimes ruthless man. He certainly knew that the land he oversaw was renowned for insurrections and for resistance to foreign customs and rule. He was determined that things would never get out of control while he was in charge.

The religious leaders accused Jesus of claiming to be a king, forbidding the people to pay taxes, riling up the people from Galilee to Jerusalem, and of many other things. Pilate asked Jesus if he was the king of the Jews. "[Jesus] answered him, 'You say so'" (Mark 15:2). Though Pilate asked Jesus about all of the other charges that were leveled against him, Jesus made no reply. Pilate was amazed.

Since Jesus was from Galilee, and since Herod (who had oversight of Galilee) was in Jerusalem at the time, Pilate sent Jesus to Herod. Herod was delighted. He had heard a good deal about Jesus, and he hoped that Jesus would perform some wondrous sign for him. This was not to be the case. Although Herod questioned him at length, Jesus made no reply. Disappointed, Herod sent Jesus back to Pilate.

Having failed in his attempt to pass the buck to Herod, and with the crowd calling for action against Jesus, Pilate hit on another solution. It was his custom each year at Passover, as a sign of good will, to release for the Jews one prisoner of their choosing. Among those in custody was a man named Barabbas, who had been arrested during an insurrection. Knowing that Jesus had been handed over to him because of the jealousy of the religious leaders, Pilate asked the crowd if he should release Jesus. But the chief priests stirred up the crowd to ask for Barabbas' release. "Pilate spoke to them again, 'Then what do you wish me to do with the man you call the King of the Jews?' They shouted back, 'Crucify him!'" (Mark 15:12-13).

Pilate had been told by his wife to "Have nothing to do with that innocent man, for today I have suffered a great deal because of a dream about him" (Matthew 27:19). With her words ringing in his ears, and seeing that a riot was in the making, Pilate took water and washed his hands before the crowd and said, "I am innocent of this man's blood; see to it yourselves" (Matthew 27:24). This was quite disingenuous on two counts. First of all, as the procurator, it was his sworn duty to uphold Roman law against the mob. Instead, he gave in to the mob. Second, the execution was to be carried out by the Roman soldiers (under his command) through crucifixion rather than by the Jewish leaders through stoning. (Two of the classic creeds of the Christian church, the Nicene Creed and the Apostles' Creed rightly include the phrase, "crucified/suffered under Pontius Pilate.")

Pilate had Jesus flogged. Then the Roman soldiers took Jesus into the courtyard of the governor's palace to mock him. They put a regal robe on him and placed a crown of thorns on his head. They struck him, spat at him, and knelt in homage before him saying, "Hail, king of the Jews!" (Mark 15:18). Having had their fun at Jesus' expense, the soldiers removed the cloak, put his own clothes on him, and led him out to be crucified.

Jesus, carrying his heavy cross, was led outside the city walls to a place called Golgotha (place of a skull). Since Jesus was weakened by the severe flogging and other mistreatment he had endured, the soldiers compelled a man named Simon of Cyrene to carry the cross.

Jesus was crucified with his hands and feet nailed to a rough wooden cross and with a placard above his head that read, "Jesus of Nazareth, the King of the Jews." Two robbers were also crucified, one on either side of Jesus. Crucifixion, the Romans' favored method of execution, was exceedingly cruel. The victim was stripped naked and left hanging in public view to be taunted by those passing by. Death was slow, ultimately coming by fatigue, muscle cramping, hunger, thirst, and asphyxiation. Crucifixion was the ultimate torture and indignity.

As Jesus hung on the cross, the soldiers cast lots to divide his clothing. Religious leaders, soldiers, and even those crucified with Jesus scoffed at him saying, "He saved others; let him save himself if he is the Messiah of God, his chosen one!" (Luke 23:35) and "Let the Messiah, the King of Israel, come down from the cross now, so that we may see and believe" (Mark 15:32).

The four gospel writers record seven words or statements that Jesus spoke as he hung dying: "Father, forgive them; for they do not know what they are doing" (Luke 23:34). "When Jesus saw his mother and the disciple whom he loved standing beside her, he said to his mother, 'Woman, here is your son.' Then he said to the disciple, 'Here is your mother'" (John 19:26-27). "Then [one of the robbers who was crucified with Jesus] said, 'Jesus, remember me when you come into your kingdom.' [Jesus] replied, 'Truly I tell you, today you will be with me in Paradise'" (Luke 23:42-43). "I am thirsty" (John 19:28). "'*Eloi, Eloi, lema sabachthani?*' which means, 'My God, my God, why have you forsaken me?'" (Mark 15:34). "Father, into your hands I commend my spirit" (Luke 23:46). "It is finished" (John 19:30).

At noon, darkness came over the land until three in the afternoon. When Jesus breathed his last, the curtain in the temple that veiled the most holy place was torn in two from the top to the bottom; and the earth shook. The centurion who stood facing Jesus said, "Truly this man was God's son!" (Mark 15:39).

Many women were there, watching from a distance. Among them were Mary Magdalene, Mary the mother of James and Joseph, and the mother of James and John.

That evening, Joseph of Arimathea (who was both a respected member of the Jewish council and a disciple of Jesus) went to Pilate and asked for the body of Jesus. Pilate, having been assured that Jesus was dead, gave Joseph permission to remove the body from the cross. Joseph and Nicodemus (whom we met earlier when he came to Jesus by night), wrapped Jesus' body in a clean linen cloth and laid it in Joseph's own new tomb which had been hewn in the rock. They rolled a huge stone across the opening and went away. Mary Magdalene and the other Mary accompanied them to see where Jesus' body had been placed.

It was their intent to bring spices and ointments and properly anoint the body when the sabbath was over.

Who, then, was responsible for the death of Jesus? Matthew tells us that when Pilate washed his hands of the whole affair, the crowd of Jews said, "His blood be on us and on our children!" (Matthew 27:25). Tragically, this verse has been used as a warrant for the persecution of the Jews throughout history. This is a terrible misapplication of the verse. As mentioned above, Pilate could not absolve himself of responsibility. Though the Jewish religious leaders did call for Jesus' death, the Romans were the ones who actually executed Jesus. Jews and Gentiles were equally culpable; and it was for the sins of all people, Jews and Gentiles alike, that Jesus went to the cross. Let it also be remembered that hatred of the Jews is irrational at best, since Jesus, his disciples, and the earliest Christians were all Jews.

On a deeper level, Satan had been waiting for an opportune time to destroy Jesus. What Satan could not accomplish through King Herod when Jesus was an infant, and what he could not bring to fruition when he tempted Jesus in the wilderness, he believed he had now been able to do. Taking advantage of the Jewish religious leaders' fears that Jesus would upset their cherished status quo or their conviction that Jesus was guilty of blasphemy, and playing on the fears of Pilate and the Roman authorities that to do other than to crucify Jesus would be to risk major unrest and violence, Satan seemed to have won.

What Satan did not know, and what passes all human understanding, is that this death of Jesus was God's plan from the beginning, to turn all things right again. The Messiah had ascended his throne.

For thought or discussion:

- What would you have done if you had been Pontius Pilate?
- Which of Jesus' sayings from the cross touches you most powerfully?
- Is there a work of art portraying the crucifixion that is especially meaningful to you?

(In church tradition and on liturgical calendars, Good Friday is two days before Easter. The liturgical color is black although red or violet can also be used. If the stripping of the altar is part of the Maundy Thursday ritual, no paraments or colored stoles are used on Good Friday.)

74. Wonder of Wonders

Easter
Matthew 28, Mark 16, Luke 24, John 20

Imagine how devastated Jesus' disciples and the women who had observed the crucifixion were when they awoke on the sabbath, and in the bright light of day, realized that the events of the previous day had not been a bad dream, but had actually occurred. Their Master was dead.

That sabbath, a high holy day, part of Passover, should have been a day of worship, rest, and renewal. For Jesus' followers, it was instead a day of grief and confusion. Their hopes and dreams had died as Jesus breathed his last. What were they to do? Where were they to go? It was a time of deep and wrenching soul-searching.

When the sabbath was over, Mary Magdalene and other women went to do the grim but loving service of anointing the body of Jesus. It was the very least they could do for this man who had so impacted their lives and who had filled them with such hope and joy. At first light, they went to the tomb; and as they went, they discussed how they could possibly move the huge stone that blocked the entrance.

To their great surprise, the stone had already been rolled back. An angel, resplendent in white, was sitting there; and the women were terrified. "But he said to them, 'Do not be alarmed; you are looking for Jesus of Nazareth, who was crucified. He has been raised; he is not here. Look, there is the place they laid him. But go, tell his disciples and Peter that he is going ahead of you to Galilee; there you will see him, just as he told you'" (Mark 16:6-7).

The women, filled with wonder and great joy, quickly left the tomb and ran to tell the disciples the glorious news. Breathlessly, they told what they had seen and heard. "But these words seemed to [the disciples] an idle tale, and they did not believe them" (Luke 24:11). Women's testimony was not deemed trustworthy in those days, and such a story was simply unimaginable. How could such a thing be true?

They had all forgotten that three times Jesus had told them, "See, we are going up to Jerusalem, and the Son of Man will be handed over to the chief priests and scribes, and they will condemn him to death; then they will hand him over to the Gentiles to be mocked and flogged and crucified; and on the third day he will be raised" (Matthew 20:18-19). They had observed the abuse and death. The sheer horror of those events had driven the final words of Jesus' prediction from their minds.

Nevertheless, just to be sure, Peter and John ran to the tomb to check it out for themselves. What they found was not merely an empty tomb, but also a sign of the verity of the testimony of the women. Entering the tomb, they saw the linen cloths in which Jesus had been wrapped lying where his body had been, and they saw the cloth that had been on Jesus' head rolled up in a place by itself. Seeing this, they believed. Jesus had indeed been raised on the third day!

Later that day, two of Jesus' followers were walking to a village called Emmaus, about seven miles from Jerusalem. As they walked, they talked with each other about the dreadful experience of the previous two days. Jesus came and walked with them, but they were kept from recognizing him. He asked them what they were discussing. They told him about the crucifixion and then sadly said, "But we had hoped that he was the one to redeem Israel" (Luke 24:21). They also told Jesus that some women of their group had been to the tomb and had returned saying they had seen a vision of angels who told them Jesus was alive. Some of the disciples had been to the tomb but did not find the body. All they knew for sure was that Jesus had been killed.

"Then [Jesus] said to them, 'Oh, how foolish you are, and how slow of heart to believe all that the prophets have declared! Was it not necessary that the Messiah should suffer these things and then enter his glory?' Then beginning with Moses and all the prophets, he interpreted to them the things about himself in all the scriptures" (Luke 24:25-27). That had to have been the ultimate Bible study lesson. Oh, to have been there!

When they came to the village of Emmaus, since it was late in the day, the two travelers urged Jesus to stay with them. As they sat down to eat, Jesus took bread and blessed and broke it for them. Immediately their eyes were opened and they recognized him. He vanished from their sight. "They said to each other, 'Were not our hearts burning within us while he was talking to us on the road, while he was opening the scriptures to us?'" (Luke 24:32). Although it was growing dark, they hurried back to Jerusalem to share this wonderful news with the disciples.

Meanwhile, the disciples had gathered behind locked doors. They were afraid that what had happened to their Master might also happen to them. Though the doors were locked, Jesus suddenly stood among them and said, "Peace be with you" (John 20:19). Imagine how stunned and bewildered they must have been, blinking their eyes in disbelief. Then he showed them the nail marks in his hands and feet and the place where a soldier had pierced his side. "While in their joy they were disbelieving and still wondering, he said to them, 'Have you anything here to eat?' They gave him a piece of broiled fish, and he took it and ate in their presence" (Luke 24:41-43). He was definitely not a ghost or a disembodied spirit. He was flesh and blood (though with a unique resurrected body), and he was alive.

Thomas, one of the twelve, was not with the other disciples when Jesus came. They told him that they had seen Jesus, but he replied, "Unless I see the mark of the nails in his hands, and put my finger in the mark of the nails and my hand in his side, I will not believe" (John 20:25). For a whole week the ten disciples reveled in Jesus' resurrection, and all week Thomas doubted. Jesus come to them again when Thomas was present. "Then he said to Thomas, 'Put your finger here and see my hands. Reach out your hand and put it in my side. Do not doubt but believe'" (John 20:27). Thomas did believe, and though he has been known throughout history as "doubting Thomas," his faith and joy were now the equal of all the other disciples.

Once crucified, dead and buried, Jesus had been raised to life again. Death could not hold him. Life was the final word, just as Jesus had said that it would be. By his death and resurrection, Jesus conquered death and opened the way to eternal life for all who believe in him.

Wonder of wonders!

For thought or discussion:

- What does the resurrection of Jesus mean for you?
- What signs have you had (or do you need) to convince you of the truth of the resurrection?
- How do you think you would have reacted if you had been with the disciples when Jesus appeared to them?

(In church tradition and on liturgical calendars, Easter/The Resurrection of Our Lord is the highest holy day. It is a movable festival. In the Western Christian church, Easter falls on the first Sunday after the first full moon occurring on or after the spring equinox; therefore, anytime between March 22 and April 25. Ash Wednesday, Holy Week, the Ascension, and Pentecost are tied to Easter and their dates move accordingly. In the Eastern Christian church, which follows a different calendar, Easter Sunday occurs later, between April 4 and May 8. The liturgical color for Easter is white.)

75. High and Lifted Up Again

The Ascension

Acts 1

In the forty days that followed Jesus' resurrection, he appeared to his disciples on a number of occasions. The first of those was the second time he came to the disciples, including Thomas, which we have already recounted.

Some days later, seven of the disciples returned to Galilee. They decided to go fishing. It proved to be a fruitless endeavor, for though they fished all night, they caught nothing. Just after sunrise, they saw a man on the beach who asked them if they had any fish. When they answered in the negative, he told them to cast their net on the righthand side of the boat. To their amazement, their net was filled with so many fish they could not haul it into the boat.

John said to Peter, "It is the Lord!" (John 21:7). At that, Peter, who was stripped for fishing, put on clothes, jumped into the water, and swam to shore. The others came in the boat, dragging the net which was filled with 153 large fish.

When they brought the boat to shore, they saw that the man was Jesus, as John had declared, and that he was cooking fish and baking bread over a charcoal fire. He invited them to breakfast. They gladly accepted his invitation, and what a joy it was to share a meal again with their Master.

After breakfast, Jesus asked Peter if he loved him. "He said to him, 'Yes, Lord; you know that I love you.' Jesus said to him, 'Feed my lambs'" (John 21:15). Twice more Jesus asked Peter this question. Perhaps this was done because Peter had three times denied that he knew Jesus. Yet there is more to this than meets the eye for anyone who reads this account in English. In the Greek language there are four primary words for love, and each has a unique meaning. Two of the four occur in this passage. The first time Jesus asked Peter the question, he used the word *agape*. This is the selfless, sacrificial, unconditional love with which God loves us. Peter responded with the word *phileo*. This is the love people generally have for one another. (The slogan for Philadelphia is "City of Brotherly Love.") *Phileo* is powerful and life-giving friendship, but it is far short of *agape*. The second question and answer also used *agape* and *phileo*. The third time Jesus used *phileo* in his question, and Peter responded with that same word. In each case, Peter was charged by Jesus, as a sign of his love, to tend the Lord's flock (people). Though Jesus' *agape* love was beyond what Peter could muster, Jesus accepted Peter and all the disciples where they were and called them to continue to follow him.

On another occasion, Jesus met with his disciples on a mountain in Galilee and gave them a command and a promise. "All authority in heaven and on earth has been given to me. Go therefore and make disciples of all nations, baptizing them in the name of the Father and of the Son and of the Holy Spirit, and teaching them to obey everything that I have commanded you. And remember, I am with you always, to the end of the age" (Matthew 28:18-20).

The apostle Paul (the subject of two of the following stories) tells us that Jesus appeared to Peter and the disciples, to more than five hundred people at one time, to James (Jesus' brother), and "Last of all, as to one untimely born, he appeared also to me" (1 Corinthians 15:8).

The final physical meeting of Jesus and his disciples occurred in Bethany, forty days after Easter. Like so many other things that the disciples experienced, this too took a totally unexpected turn.

The disciples began by asking Jesus something that had been on their minds. "Lord, is this the time when you will restore the kingdom to Israel?" (1:6). Three years of earthly ministry had been followed by a most surprising week in Jerusalem. No doubt the disciples (and many other people as well) were of the opinion that when Jesus entered Jerusalem on that Palm Sunday, he was there to ascend the throne of David. As far as they could tell, even though that week had been full of both agony and wonder, the kingdom had not been restored. Forty more days had passed. Was now the time for Jesus to ascend his throne and to usher in his glorious reign?

"He replied, 'It is not for you to know the times or periods that the Father has set by his own authority. But you will receive power when the Holy Spirit has come upon you; and you will be my witnesses in Jerusalem, in all Judea and Samaria, and to the ends of the earth'" (1:7-8). They were still confused about the nature of the kingdom that Jesus had come to establish. Nevertheless, they had been given their marching orders.

Then, adding amazement to their confusion, Jesus was lifted up before their eyes and ascended into the heavens until a cloud blocked him from their sight. They stood dumbfounded, gazing into the sky. Suddenly, two men in white robes appeared to them and said, "Men of Galilee, why do you stand looking up toward heaven? This Jesus, who has been taken up from you into heaven, will come in the same way as you saw him go into heaven" (1:11).

They could not have imagined or expected this ascension any more than they had imagined or expected the resurrection. Would the surprises never stop? Why had he left them? When would he be coming again? Was he serious about them being his witnesses in Jerusalem, let alone to the ends of the earth? And what was this Holy Spirit that was to come upon them? Perhaps they remembered that he had said to them that he would not leave them orphaned and that "the Advocate, the Holy Spirit, whom the Father will send in my name, will teach you everything, and remind you of all that I have said to you" (John 14:26).

They returned to Jerusalem to ponder these things and to await what would come next.

For thought or discussion:

- How much strength and comfort do you think the disciples experienced each time they saw Jesus after his resurrection?
- What would you have been feeling if you had been with the disciples when Jesus ascended?
- Do you think that Jesus wants you to be his witness right where you are?

(In church tradition and on liturgical calendars, The Ascension of Our Lord is celebrated on a Thursday, forty days after Easter Sunday. The liturgical color for the Ascension is white.)

76. Rushing Wind and Breath of God

Pentecost

Acts 2

Waiting can be hard. The future will not come any sooner by our being anxious, but all too often our waiting is marked by impatience. The disciples had been told by Jesus to wait for the promised Holy Spirit. They waited, day after day.

As they waited, they spent a great deal of time in prayer. Mary, Jesus' mother, and his brothers and others joined with the disciples so that those who gathered together numbered about 120.

One piece of business to which the disciples attended was the selection of a replacement for Judas. The criteria for the one who would again make the number of disciples twelve was that he had to be one who had accompanied the disciples from the beginning, "from the baptism of John until the day when he was taken up from us — one of these must become a witness with us to his resurrection" (1:22). A man named Matthias was chosen.

What happened next, was in no way business as usual.

The climactic events of Jesus' life (his death and resurrection) had occurred in Jerusalem during Passover. Once again, pilgrims came to the holy city for Shavout, the Feast of Weeks or the Festival of Harvest or Firstfruits. This gathering marked the harvesting of the wheat, and it was also a time to commemorate God's covenant relationship with Israel. This Jewish celebration, fifty days after Passover, was also called Pentecost. Jewish people who had been scattered into many countries came for the festival, and they came speaking many languages.

On the day of Pentecost, when the believers were gathered in one place, suddenly with the sound of rushing wind, the breath of God, the Holy Spirit, swept over them. "Divided tongues, as of fire, appeared among them, and a tongue rested on each of them. All of them were filled with the Holy Spirit and began to speak in other languages, as the Spirit gave them ability" (2:3-4). This drew a crowd.

Imagine the amazement of the people as they heard, in their own native languages, this proclamation of the mighty acts of God. The crowd was astonished, for it was evident that those who were speaking were all Galileans, and yet what reached the ears of each listener were words spoken in his or her mother tongue. (There is something powerfully comforting about hearing one's own language when in a foreign place.)

While the majority of the hearers were amazed that "in our own languages we hear them speaking about God's deeds of power," (2:11) there were some who dismissed what they were hearing as the babbling of drunken men.

Peter stepped to the fore and addressed the crowd. He said that those who had been speaking were not drunk, but that this was the fulfillment of the words of the Old Testament prophet Joel. "In the last days it will be, God declares, that I will pour out my Spirit upon all flesh, and your sons and your daughters shall prophesy, and your young men shall see visions, and your old men shall dream dreams…Then everyone who calls on the name of the Lord shall be saved" (2:17 and 21). The promised gift of the Holy Spirit had indeed been given to the believers, and God was at work to bring salvation to all who would hear.

Peter went on to preach to the people about Jesus of Nazareth who had been crucified and raised to life. "This Jesus God raised up, and of that all of us are witnesses. Being therefore exalted at the right hand of God, and having received from the Father the promise of the Holy Spirit, he has poured out this that you both see and hear…Therefore let the entire house of Israel know with certainty that God has made him both Lord and Messiah, this Jesus whom you crucified" (2:32-33, 36).

Peter's sermon was not lengthy, but it was powerful. Many in the crowd asked what they needed to do in response. Peter told them to repent (to turn from their old ways) and to be baptized, "so that your sins may be forgiven; and you will receive the gift of the Holy Spirit" (2:38). He went on to say that this promise of life in Jesus was for them, for their children, and for people near and far whom the Lord would call. Devout Jews were being called by God to believe in and to follow Jesus, their Messiah. About 3,000 people responded in faith and were baptized that day. "They devoted themselves to the apostles' teaching and fellowship, to the breaking of bread and the prayers" (2:42).

One of the amazing things about this new community of believers was their love for each other. They pooled their resources so that no one was needy. They shared meals with thankful and generous hearts, and they spent time together in the temple praising God. Because of their joy-filled example, day after day other people were drawn to Jesus and were numbered among those who were saved.

Where the Holy Spirit is present, love and care and faith and joy are sure to be also.

For thought or discussion:

- Has there been an occasion when you found it difficult to wait for a promise's fulfillment?
- Have you experienced the Holy Spirit at work in your life?
- What traits do you think should characterize those who follow Jesus and have received the Holy Spirit?

(In church tradition and on liturgical calendars, The Day of Pentecost is celebrated on the seventh Sunday after Easter Sunday. The liturgical color for The Day of Pentecost is red.)

77. Blinding Light and Falling Scales

Conversion of Saul/Paul
Acts 9

Ananias was given an assignment that would make even the bravest man quake in his sandals. To understand why, it is critical to understand the story of Saul/Paul.

We first meet Saul of Tarsus at the end of the seventh chapter of Acts. He stood by watching and approving as others stoned to death a man named Stephen. Stephen was one of the seven men the disciples had chosen to be deacons and to oversee the physical needs of the growing Christian community. Stephen powerfully proclaimed Jesus as Lord and Messiah, and for this he was brought before the council and charged with stirring up the people and with blasphemy. His words before the council so riled up the crowd that they put him to death.

This began a period of persecution of Christians in Jerusalem and led to the dispersion of believers throughout Judea and Samaria. Saul was at the forefront of this war against the Way (as the followers of Jesus were first called), going into homes of Christians and hauling them to prison. So zealous was Saul that fear of him spread among the believers.

Saul was a Jew from Tarsus in Cilicia and was therefore also a Roman citizen by birth. He was brought up in Jerusalem and studied at the feet of Gamaliel (a noted Pharisee and rabbi). Saul was a Pharisee who was zealous for God and for the traditions of Israel.

In his zeal for persecuting followers of the Way, Saul, bearing letters from the high priest, set out for Damascus to find believers there and to bring them bound to Jerusalem. At midday, as he neared Damascus, an intensely bright light flashed around him. "He fell to the ground and heard a voice saying to him, 'Saul, Saul, why do you persecute me?' He asked, 'Who are you, Lord?' The reply came, 'I am Jesus, whom you are persecuting. But get up and enter the city, and you will be told what you are to do'" (9:4-6). Saul was struck blind, and so his companions took him by the hand and led him the rest of the way to Damascus. There for three days, he could see nothing, and he neither ate nor drank. He who had been so powerful and determined, was now helpless and uncertain. Was Jesus punishing him or testing him? What was to be?

The Lord appeared to Ananias in a vision and told him to go to Straight Street, to the home of a man named Judas, and there to find Saul of Tarsus. He was to lay his hands on Saul to restore Saul's sight. As you would imagine, Ananias' response was to strongly question the wisdom of such a venture. He had heard about Saul, and he knew that Saul had come to Damascus specifically to find and to arrest Christians. How was Ananias to know that this was not a devious ploy on Saul's part?

The Lord said, "Go, for he is an instrument whom I have chosen to bring my name before Gentiles and kings and before the people of Israel; I myself will show him how much he must suffer for the sake of my name" (9:15-16). The Lord also told Ananias that Saul had been praying and had seen in a vision that someone would come to restore him.

Ananias went (likely with a full measure of trepidation), and entering the house, he laid his hands on Saul and said, "Brother Saul, the Lord Jesus, who appeared to you on your way here, has sent me so that you may regain your sight and be filled with the Holy Spirit" (9:17). Immediately something like scales fell from Saul's eyes and his sight was restored. He got up, was baptized, ate, and was filled with both strength and the Holy Spirit.

In the days that followed, Saul was with the followers of the Way in Damascus; and he proclaimed Jesus in the synagogues, saying, "He is the Son of God" (9:20). His testimony became ever bolder and more powerful. Many who heard him were amazed, for they said, "Is not this the man who made havoc in Jerusalem among those who invoked this name?" (9:21).

So convincing was Saul's preaching that some of the Jewish leaders sought to kill him, and they watched the city gates so that they might seize him. Saul's friends, however, lowered him in a basket through an opening in the wall at night so that he could leave Damascus safely.

As time passed, Saul connected with the believers in Jerusalem. Again, he needed to convince them that he who had persecuted Jesus' followers was now himself a devout follower of Jesus. In fact, Saul, whose name was later changed to Paul*, became the foremost apostle of Jesus. He traveled widely, establishing church after church, and risking his life to make known the good news of Jesus. (More about that later.)

Saul/Paul was learned and bright and articulate and zealous. The same qualities that made him a powerful enemy of the Way also made him a powerful advocate for it. His conversion to Jesus did not make him renounce his learning or his wisdom or his energy but to use these very things to make the case for Jesus as the Messiah and as the Savior of the world. To follow Jesus is not to stop thinking but to think differently, viewing the world through Jesus' eyes, caring for the world and all its inhabitants with Jesus' heart, and seeking to think Jesus' thoughts after him.

For thought or discussion:

- Have you ever had an assignment that, like Ananias, caused you fear for your life or safety?
- Has there been a time in your life when you made a complete turnaround in your thinking?
- What unique gifts has God given you to enable you to speak and to act in Jesus' name?

* The name Paul is first used in Acts 13:9 and then throughout the remainder of Acts and in all his letters to the early churches. He is always referred to by that name now, and never as Saul.

78. Who Is In and Who Is Out?

Peter and Cornelius
Acts 10

The earliest followers of Jesus were all Jews. Since they understood themselves to be God's chosen people, there was a tendency for those early believers to conclude that Jesus, the Messiah, fulfilling centuries of prophecy, had come for them alone.

That conviction was put to the test when an angel appeared to a man named Cornelius. Cornelius was a Roman centurion living in Caesarea. "He was a devout man who feared God with all his household; he gave alms generously to the people and prayed constantly to God" (10:2). Alas, the fact that Cornelius was a good man did not negate the fact that he was a Gentile and so was not numbered among the chosen people.

One day when he was praying, an angel came to Cornelius in a vision and told him that his prayers and alms had been received by God. He was instructed to send for Simon Peter who was at that time staying in Joppa with another Simon in a house beside the sea. In response, Cornelius sent two of his servants and a devout soldier under his command to find Peter.

The following day, at noon, Peter was on the roof of the house in Joppa. He was praying while food was being prepared. He too had a vision. Something like a large sheet was being lowered from heaven, held by its four corners. In it were all sorts of reptiles, birds, and four-footed creatures. "Then he heard a voice saying, 'Get up, Peter; kill and eat.' But Peter said, 'By no means, Lord; for I have never eaten anything that is profane or unclean.' The voice said to him again, a second time, 'What God has made clean, you must not call profane'" (10:13-15). Two more times this was repeated.

While Peter was trying to make sense of this vision, the three men sent by Cornelius arrived. The Spirit instructed Peter to speak with the men and to do as they requested. Therefore, the next morning, accompanied by some of the believers in Joppa, Peter set out with the three men to travel to Caesarea.

The next day, when they came to the home of Cornelius, they found that he had gathered a group of his relatives and friends to hear what Peter would have to say. The first thing that Peter said to the assembled crowd was, "You yourselves know that it is unlawful for a Jew to associate with or to visit a Gentile; but God has shown me that I should not call anyone profane or unclean. When I was sent for, I came without objection. Now may I ask why you sent for me?" (10:28-29).

Cornelius told about the angelic visitation he had experienced four days earlier and about his response to that vision. "So now all of us are here in the presence of God to listen to all that the Lord has commanded you to say" (10:33). Peter said, "I truly understand that God shows no partiality, but in every nation anyone who fears him and does what is right is acceptable to him" (10:34-35). Then he told them about Jesus, recounting his life, ministry, death, and resurrection. He concluded, "[Jesus] commanded us to preach to the people and to testify that he is the one ordained by God as judge of the living and the dead. All the prophets testify about him that everyone who believes in him receives forgiveness of sins through his name" (10:42-43).

As Peter was speaking, the Holy Spirit came on those who were listening, and they began to praise God. Those who had come with Peter were astonished that God had given the Holy Spirit even to Gentiles. Peter exclaimed, "Can anyone withhold the water for baptizing these people who have received the Holy Spirit just as we have?" (10:47). So Cornelius and those gathered with him were baptized. Peter and his fellow Jewish believers then remained in Caesarea with Cornelius and the other Gentile believers for several days.

Although there were yet times when Peter seemed to forget the truth of his thrice-seen vision of the sheet and creatures, this visit to Cornelius made God's intent crystal clear. The message of life and salvation in Jesus Christ is meant for all who will believe, Jew and Gentile alike. All stand on level ground before God, and God desires that all should come to know the love and grace that have been made available equally to all people in Jesus.

For thought or discussion:

- What biases or prejudices do you have toward other groups, races, or classes of people?
- In what ways has God's word challenged those biases or prejudices for you?
- What do you think it means when it says that "God shows no partiality"?

79. Making Known the Unknown

Paul in Athens
Acts 17

Paul (formerly Saul) became the foremost apostle to the Gentiles. He made three extensive missionary journeys in the countries of Cyprus, Syria, Asia Minor, Macedonia, and Greece. He also traveled to Rome, proclaiming Jesus as Lord in that city and at each stop on the way from Jerusalem to Rome.

Initially, his practice was to go to the synagogue(s) in the cities he visited. There he preached about Jesus being the long-awaited Messiah, explaining from the scriptures how Jesus was the fulfillment of God's promises. Some who heard him responded positively, but others rejected his message. When some of the latter became increasingly hostile, even to the point of violence against Paul, he focused his proclamation on the Gentiles.

Paul stayed in some of the cities for a few years and in others for a very short time. In each case, having gathered a group of believers, he appointed leaders to carry on the work of the faith community after his departure. On his first journey, he was accompanied by Barnabas. On his second journey, Silas and Timothy were his primary companions. On the third journey, Paul was not joined by any single individual but by various believers along the way. Whenever possible, Paul revisited the churches he had founded to encourage and strengthen the believers in each place. He also wrote letters for the same purpose.

When Paul was in Athens, he was deeply troubled by the vast number of idols he observed in the city. He preached in the synagogue to the Jews and in the marketplace to all who were there, proclaiming the good news of Jesus' resurrection. He also debated with Epicurean and Stoic philosophers who were, by and large, intrigued enough to want to know more about this new teaching. "Now all the Athenians and the foreigners living there would spend their time in nothing but telling or hearing something new" (17:21). Paul was therefore invited to speak to those gathered at the Areopagus.

Paul was a master at meeting people where they were so that he had a foundation for sharing the news of Jesus. Here was a perfect example. He began by complimenting those assembled for being religious, as evidenced by the multitude of objects of worship in Athens. He said that he had even found an altar inscribed, "To an unknown god." While this may have been erected by the Athenians to be sure that they had not overlooked (and offended) a god, this became a perfect jumping off point for Paul.

"What therefore you worship as unknown, this I proclaim to you. The God who made the world and everything in it, he who is Lord of heaven and earth, does not live in shrines made by human hands…he made all nations to inhabit the whole earth… so that they would search for God and perhaps grope for him and find him — though indeed he is not far from each of us. For 'in him we live and move and have our being'" (17:23-28). Paul continued by urging his hearers to turn from ignorance and idolatry to the living God, whom he was making known to them and who had revealed his power and eternal purposes by raising Jesus from the dead.

As was always the case when Paul proclaimed the story of Jesus, there were some who scoffed and dismissed his message and others who wanted to know more. Some became followers of Jesus and joined the ranks of the Christians, living in and sharing the good news.

Remember that when God had sent Ananias to restore Paul's sight as part of his conversion experience on the road to Damascus, God had said to Ananias, "I myself will show him how much he must suffer for the sake of my name" (Acts 9:16). While the encounter in Athens did not involve suffering, Paul's visits to many other places involved great difficulties. In the second letter Paul wrote to the church in Corinth, in the eleventh chapter, he gave a catalog of the trials he endured. Life as an apostle for Jesus was anything but easy, but because of the Holy Spirit at work in Paul, and because of the reality of God's call to this ministry, Paul's journeys were incredibly fruitful.

Before his Ascension, Jesus told his disciples, "But you will receive power when the Holy Spirit has come upon you; and you will be my witnesses in Jerusalem, in all Judea and Samaria, and to the ends of the earth" (Acts 1:8). The first disciples focused their attention on Judea and Samaria, but it was Paul who began the process of carrying the message to the ends of the earth.

For thought or discussion:

- Why is it important in communication to know the other person's experiences and context?
- Is sharing a message a failure if not everyone who hears receives it positively?
- When did the word of Jesus first come to your particular "end of the earth"?

80. Plagues and Beasts and Dragons, O My!

Revelation
Revelation

At the end of the Bible is the book of Revelation, and it is perhaps the most misunderstood of all the 66 books.

Like the book of Daniel in the Old Testament, Revelation is apocalyptic literature. It is filled with imagery, and the reader needs to decipher those images to make sense of the meaning. While most apocalyptic literature is written under a pseudonym, the writer of this book is the apostle John as it says.

John was imprisoned on Patmos, a Greek island off the coast of Asia Minor (present-day Turkey). He wanted to send a letter of encouragement to the Christians who were in the throes of persecution under Emperor Domitian. Had he stated that Rome's days were numbered, and that God would sweep away the emperor and all his minions, it is unlikely that his jailers would have allowed his writing to leave the island. Therefore, he wrote about the overthrow of Babylon, a civilization moldering in the dust of history. He spoke of visions, plagues, beasts, dragons, and the forces of Satan. His writing likely seemed to be the harmless ramblings of a man losing touch with reality. But in fact, this Revelation of John echoed the message of the previous 65 books, and it contained the same good news. God's kingdom is eternal and all other powers will pass away.

The two major misunderstandings of Revelation relate to history and to the limiting of God's power and rule.

While Revelation does deal with the end of history and is also a timeless word, it needs to be understood, first of all, in its own time and context. The book is not intended to reveal the date of the end of time. It is not as if by determining where we now are in the book, we can predict the end date. Jesus himself said that "it is not for you to know the times or periods that the Father has set by his own authority" (Acts 1:7). Instead, we need to listen to both the challenge and the encouragement that John sets before us, as we live in these days.

As to the matter of limitations, John does speak of 140,000 elect who are to be saved and of a thousand-year reign of Christ.

Understanding eastern numerology, however, leads to the conviction that these numbers are figurative rather than literal, expansive rather than limiting. Multiplying by ten is to speak of expansiveness, so 12,000 from each of the twelve tribes is actually twelve times twelve times ten times ten times ten. Those to be saved are beyond our imagining. So too, Christ's reign is without limitation but goes on for all eternity. "'I am the Alpha and the Omega,' says the Lord God, who is and who was and who is to come, the almighty" (1:8).

Another example of the symbolic use of numbers is the number of the beast, 666. Attempts have been made throughout history to make this number fit a host of hated people. The number of divinity is seven; that of humanity is six. So what John is saying is that the antichrist, anyone claiming to be divine or worthy of worship, is actually deceiving people. For that person is human, human, human (six, six, six).

Then there are the seven seals and the seven trumpets and the seven bowls of the wrath of God. Does this mean that there are 21 devastations to come, one after the other? More likely, remembering Peter's vision of the sheet filled with unclean creatures let down from heaven three times, John wrote of seven devastations and then repeated it two more times with different images for emphasis.

So then, what is the point of this final book of the Bible? There are three key themes. The first is a call to patient endurance for those who are suffering for their faith in Jesus. John tells them not to lose hope but to remember Gods' steadfast love and faithful deliverance of his beloved throughout history. The second, as witnessed by Jesus' words to the seven churches in Asia Minor, is that God chastens those whom he loves. In so far as the believers thought of themselves as holy on their own, they were reminded of their imperfections in faith, hope, and love and of God's desire to make them perfect. Being disciplined is often painful, but love requires it. God will settle for nothing less than perfecting those who belong to him. The third, and the most important theme, echoed on page after page of Revelation, is that God is in control and can be absolutely trusted. The lamb (Jesus, by whose death and resurrection the kingdom has been opened to all believers) is on the throne. Those in God's presence worship him without ceasing. The key verse of Revelation is this: "Then I heard what seemed to be the voice of a great multitude, like the sound of many waters and like the sound of mighty thunderpeals, crying out, 'Hallelujah! For the Lord our God the almighty reigns'" (19:6).

The final two chapters of Revelation bring us to the New Jerusalem and to the restoration of all things. The Bible began in the Garden of Eden where the tree of life was in its midst and where all things were in perfect harmony. The Bible ends in the holy city where the tree of life is in its midst and where everything is in perfect harmony.

"And I heard a loud voice from the throne saying, 'See, the home of God is among mortals. He will dwell with them; they will be his peoples, and God himself will be with them; he will wipe every tear from their eyes. Death will be no more; mourning and crying and pain will be no more, for the first things have passed away,' And the one who was seated on the throne said, 'See, I am making all things new.' Also, he said, 'Write this, for these words are trustworthy and true.' Then he said to me, 'It is done! I am the Alpha and the Omega, the beginning and the end'" (21:3-6).

God will make all things new. Then those whom he has redeemed, people beyond our numbering or imagining, will find themselves in God's presence, either at their individual deaths or at the end of the age (whenever God chooses to bring that about). There they will know the fullness of life, love, and joy; and they will forever be caught up in wonder anew.

For thought or discussion:

- How does John's proclamation that God is in control give you hope in your present situation?
- In what ways do you tend to limit God and his grace and love for you?
- Where have you discovered wonder in these stories?

Soli Deo Gloria